Business Model
YOU

Published by John Wiley & Sons, Inc., Hoboken, New Jersey.
Published simultaneously in Canada.

For general information on our other products and services or for technical support, please contact our Customer Care Department within the United States at (800) 762-2974, outside the United States at (317) 572-3993 or fax (317) 572-4002.

Wiley also publishes its books in a variety of electronic formats. Some content that appears in print may not be available in electronic books. For more information about Wiley products, visit our Web site at www.wiley.com.

ISBN 978-1-118-15631-5 (paper)
ISBN 978-1-118-22599-8 (ebk)
ISBN 978-1-118-23931-5 (ebk)

Printed in the United States of America
10 9 8 7 6 5 4 3 2 1

COVER ILLUSTRATION BY
Matt Hammill
www.matthammill.com

ADDITIONAL ILLUSTRATIONS BY
Alan Smith

STILL LIFE PHOTOGRAPHY BY
Trish Papadakos

Business Model

YOU

A One-Page
Method
for Reinventing
Your Career

WRITTEN BY
Tim Clark, in collaboration
with Alexander Osterwalder
and Yves Pigneur

DESIGNED BY
Alan Smith and Trish Papadakos

EDITED BY
Megan Lacey

PRODUCTION ASSISTANCE
Patrick van der Pijl

CO-CREATED BY
328 work-life wizards
from 43 countries

WILEY

John Wiley & Sons, Inc.

Co-created by 328 work life wizards . . .

Throughout the book, you'll notice references to "Forum members" — early readers of *Business Model You* who helped with its creation. They critiqued draft chapters, offered examples and insights, and supported the effort throughout production. Their pictures appear in the front pages, and their names appear below.[1]

Adie Shariff
Afroz Ali
AJ Shah
Alan Scott
Alan Smith
Alejandro Lembo
Alessandro De Sanctis
Alexander Osterwalder
Alfredo Osorio Asenjo
Ali Heathfield
Allan Moura Lima
Allen Miner
Amber Lewis
Andi Roberts
Andre Malzoni dos Santos Dias
Andrew E. Nixon
Andrew Warner
Anne McCrossan
Annemarie Ehren
Annette Mason
Ant Clay
Anthony Caldwell
Anthony Moore
Anton de Gier
Anton de Wet
Antonio Lucena de Faria
Beau Braund
Ben Carey

Ben White
Bernd Nurnberger
Bernie Maloney
Bertil Schaart
Björn Kijl
Blanca Vergara
Bob Fariss
Brenda Eichelberger
Brian Ruder
Brigitte Roujol
Bruce Hazen
Bruce MacVarish
Brunno Pinto Guedes Cruz
Bryan Aulick
Bryan Lubic
Camilla van den Boom
Carl B. Skompinski
Carl D'Agostino
Carles Esquerre Victori
Carlos Jose Perez Ferrer
Caroline Cleland
Cassiano Farani
Catharine MacIntosh
Cesar Picos
Charles W. Clark
Cheenu Srinivasan
Cheryl Rochford
Christian Labezin

Christian Schneider
Christine Thompson
Cindy Cooper
Claas Peter Fischer
Claire Fallon
Claudio D'Ipolitto
Császár Csaba
Daniel E. Huber
Daniel Pandza
Daniel Sonderegger
Danijel Brener
Danilo Tic
Darcy Walters-Robles
Dave Crowther
Dave Wille
David Devasahayam Edwin
David Hubbard
David Sluis
Deborah Burkholder
Deborah Mills-Scofield
Denise Taylor
Diane Mermigas
Dinesh Neelay
Diogo Carmo
Donald McMichael
Dora Luz González Bañales
Doug Gilbert
Doug Morwood

Doug Newdick
Dr. Jerry A. Smith
Dustin Lee Watson
Ed Voorhaar
Edgardo Vazquez
Eduardo Pedreño
Edwin Kruis
Eileen Bonner
Elie Besso
Elizabeth Topp
Eltje Huisman
Emmanuel A. Simon
Eric Anthony Spieth
Eric Theunis
Erik A. Leonavicius
Erik Kiaer
Erik Silden
Ernest Buise
Ernst Houdkamp
Eugen Rodel
Evert Jan van Hasselt
Fernando Saenz-Marrero
Filipe Schuur
Floris Kimman
Floris Venneman
Fran Moga
Francisco Barragan
Frank Penkala

Fred Coon
Fred Jautzus
Freek Talsma
Frenetta A. Tate
Frits Oukes
Gabriel Shalom
Gary Percy
Geert van Vlijmen
Gene Browne
Ginger Grant, PhD
Giorgio Casoni
Giorgio Pauletto
Giselle Della Mea
Greg Krauska
Greg Loudoun
Hank Byington
Hans Schriever
Hansrudolf Suter
Heiner Kaufmann
Hind
IJsbrand Kaper
Iñigo Irizar
Ioanna Matsouli
Ivo Frielink
Iwan Müller
Jacco Hiemstra
James C. Wylie
James Fyles

Jan Schmiedgen
Jason Mahoney
Javier Guevara
Jean Gasen
Jeffrey Krames
Jelle Bartels
Jenny L. Berger
Jeroen Bosman
Joeri de Vos
Joeri Lefévre
Johan Ploeg
Johann Gevers
Johannes Frühmann
John Bardos
John van Beek
John Wark
John L. Warren
John Ziniades
Jonas Ørts Holm
Jonathan L. York
Joost de Wit
Joost Fluitsma
Jordi Collell
Juerg H. Hilgarth-Weber
Justin Coetsee
Justin Junier
Kadena Tate
Kai Kollen

Kamal Hassan
Karin van Geelen
Karl Burrow
Katarzyna Krolak-Wyszynska
Katherine Smith
Keiko Onodera
Keith Hampson
Kevin Fallon
Khushboo Chabria
Klaes Rohde Ladeby
Kuntal Trivedi
Lacides R. Castillo
Lambert Becks
Laura Stepp
Laurence Kuek Swee Seng
Lauri Kutinlahti
Lawrence Traa
Lee Heathfield
Lenny van Onselen
Linda Bryant
Liviu Ionescu
Lukas Feuerstein
Luzi von Salis
Maaike Doyer
Maarten Bouwhuis
Maarten Koomans
Manuel Grassler
Marc McLaughlin

Marcelo Salim
Marcia Kapustin
Marco van Gelder
Margaritis Malioris
Maria Augusta Orofino
Marieke Post
Marieke Versteeg
Marijn Mulders
Marjo Nieuwenhuijse
Mark Attaway
Mark Eckhardt
Mark Fritz
Mark Lundy
Mark Nieuwenhuizen
Markus Heinen
Martin Howitt
Martin Kaczynski
Marvin Sutherland
Mats Pettersson
Matt Morscheck
Matt Stormont
Matthijs Bobeldijk
Megan Lacey
Melissa Cooley
Michael Dila
Michael Eales
Michael Estabrook
Michael Korver

Michael N. Wilkens
Michael S. Ruzzi
Michael Weiss
Mikael Fuhr
Mike Lachapelle
Miki Imazu
Mikko Mannila
Mohamad Khawaja
Natasja la Lau
Nathalie Ménard
Nathan Robert Mol
Nathaniel Spohn
Nei Grando
Niall Daly
Nick Niemann
Nicolas De Santis
Oliver Buecken
Olivier J. Vavasseur
Orhan Gazi Kandemir
Paola Valeri
Patrick Betz
Patrick Keenan
Patrick Quinn
Patrick Robinson
Patrick van der Pijl
Paul Hobcraft
Paul Merino
Paula Asinof

Pere Losantos
Peter Gaunt
Peter Quinlan
Peter Schreck
Peter Sims
Peter Squires
Petrick de Koning
Philip Galligan
Philippe De Smit
Philippe Rousselot
Pieter van den Berg
PK Rasam
Rahaf Harfoush
Rainer Bareiß
Ralf de Graaf
Ralf Meyer
Ravinder S. Sethi
Raymond Guyot
Rebecca Cristina C Bulhoes
Silva
Reiner Walter
Renato Nobre
Riaz Peter
Richard Bell
Richard Gadberry
Richard Narramore
Richard Schieferdecker
Rien Dijkstra

Robert van Kooten
Rocky Romero
Roland Wijnen
Rory O'Connor
Rudolf Greger
Sang-Yong Chung (Jay)
Sara Coene
Scott Doniger
Scott Gillespie
Scott J. Propp
Sean Harry
Sean S. Kohles, PhD
Sebastiaan Terlouw
Shaojian Cao
Simon Kavanagh
Simone Veldema
Sophie Brown
Steve Brooks
Steven Forth
Steven Moody
Stewart Marshall
Stuart Woodward
Sune Klok Gudiksen
Sylvain Montreuil
Symon Jagersma
Tania Hess
Tatiana Maya Valois
Tom Yardley

Thomas Drake
Thomas Klimek
Thomas Røhr Kristiansen
Thorsten Faltings
Tiffany Rashel
Till Kraemer
Tim Clark
Tim Kastelle
Toni Borsattino
Tony Fischer
Travis Cannon
Trish Papadakos
Tufan Karaca
Ugo Merkli
Uta Boesch
Veronica Torras
Vicki Lind
Vincent de Jong
Ying Zhao-Chau
Yves Claude Aubert
Yves Pigneur

. . . from 43 countries

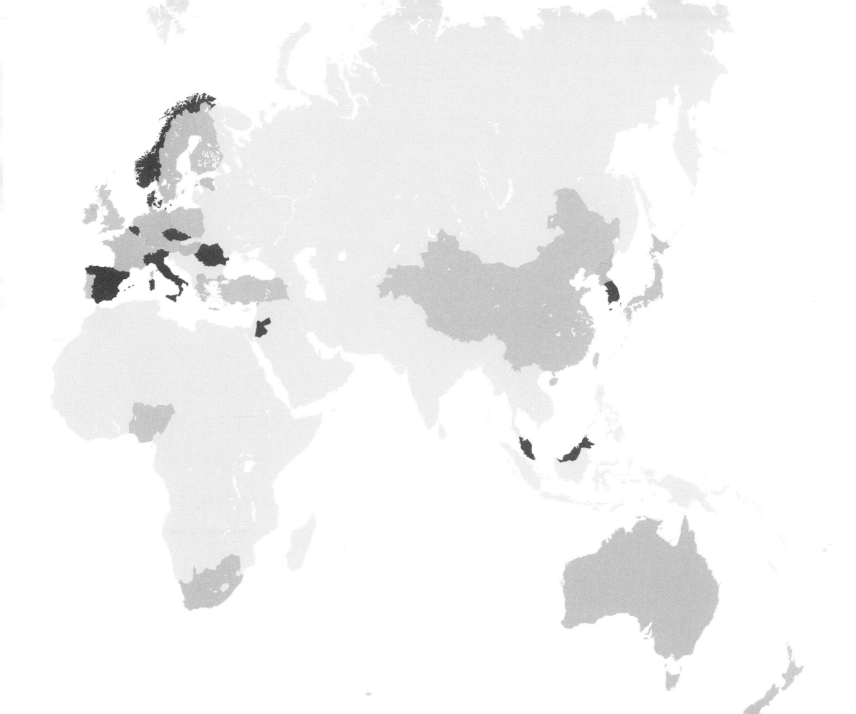

Real Reinventors:

1

Canvas

Learn to use the key tool for describing and analyzing organizational and personal business models.

2

Reflect

Revisit your life direction and consider how you want to align your personal and career aspirations.

3 Revise

Adjust — or reinvent — your work life using the Canvas and discoveries from previous sections.

4 Act

Learn to make it all happen.

5 Extras

Read more about the people and resources behind *Business Model You*.

Canvas

Learn to use the key tool for describing and analyzing organizational and personal business models.

CHAPTER 1
Business Model Thinking: Adapting to a Changing World

Why Business Model Thinking Is the Best Way For You to Adapt to a Changing World

Let's take a wild guess: You're reading this book because you've given some thought to changing your career.

You're in good company. According to one survey, five out of six adults in North America are considering changing jobs.[2] And according to our co-creators (who represent 43 countries), it's like this across the globe.

Many of us, though, lack a structured way to think about the complex and — let's face it — messy subject of switching careers. We need a simple, powerful approach — one in tune with the modern workscape and our personal needs.

Enter the business model: an excellent framework by which to describe, analyze, and reinvent a career.

No doubt you've heard the term *business model* before. What is it, exactly?

At the most basic economic level, a business model is **the logic by which an organization sustains itself financially**.[3]

As the term suggests, it ordinarily describes businesses. Our approach, however, asks you to consider *yourself* a one-person business. Then, it helps you define and modify your "personal business model" — the way you engage your strengths and talents to grow personally and professionally.

Changing Times, Changing Business Models

Much of today's job market turbulence is driven by factors beyond our personal control: recession, sweeping demographic changes, intensifying global competition, environmental issues, and so forth.

These changes are also beyond the control of most enterprises — but they profoundly affect the business models that companies use.

Because they can't change the *environment* they operate in, companies must change their *business models* (and sometimes create new ones) in order to remain competitive.

As it turns out, these new business models themselves disrupt and cause change. That creates new opportunities for some workers and unemployment for others.

Consider some examples.

Remember Blockbuster Video? It declared bankruptcy after Netflix and Redbox showed they could do a better job delivering movies and games to Customers through mail, the Internet, and vending machines.

The emergence of a new business model can affect companies in other industries, as well.

For instance, Netflix has more than 20 million customers who, thanks to the Internet, can watch television programs on computers or game consoles at any time of day or night — while skipping the advertisements. Imagine what this means for a television broadcasting industry funded by advertisers who buy time slots on the decades-old premises that: (1) ads will be embedded in programming broadcast to huge audiences at certain days and times, and (2) television-viewing audiences cannot filter out ads.

The Internet has also transformed business models in other sectors, such as music, advertising, retail, and publishing (without the Internet, this book would have been impossible to produce).

Executive recruiting firms, for example, traditionally depended on highly skilled, full-time employees who made hundreds of phone calls each week and

New business models are altering workplaces everywhere, in for-profit and nonprofit sectors alike. Enterprises must constantly evaluate and change their business models to survive.

flew cross-country to meet prospective recruits for lunch. Today the recruiting industry is dramatically different; in many cases, part-time workers, who scour Web sites from home, have replaced full-time employees.

People Must Change, Too

We're not claiming that people are the same as companies. But here's an important parallel: You, like many companies, are affected by environmental and economic factors beyond your control.

That being the case, how can you maintain success and satisfaction? You must identify how you operate — and then adapt your approach to fit changing environments.

The skills you'll learn from *Business Model You* — how to describe and think clearly about business models — will give you the power to do that.

Being able to **understand and describe your organization's business model** helps you understand how your organization can succeed, especially in turbulent economic times. Employees who care about the success of the enterprise as a whole (and know how to achieve it) are the most valuable workers — and candidates for better positions.

Once you see how a business model applies to where you work now — and where you fit within that model — you'll be able to **use the same powerful way of thinking to define, sharpen, and grow your own career**. Starting in Chapter 3, you'll define *your* personal business model. And as your career progresses, you'll be able to use *Business Model You* strategies to adjust your model and adapt to changing times.

Reading *Business Model You* will give you a distinct advantage, because while many workers define and document organizational business *practices*, few formally define or document organizational business *models*. Even fewer individuals apply the power of business model thinking to their own careers.

CHAPTER 2
The Business Model Canvas

We defined "business model"
as *the logic by which an
enterprise sustains itself
financially*. Put simply,
it's *the logic by which an
enterprise earns its livelihood.*

You might think of a business model as a blueprint describing how an organization operates.

Just as an architect prepares blueprints to guide the construction of a building, an entrepreneur designs a business model to guide the creation of an enterprise. A manager also might sketch a business model to help visualize how an existing organization operates.

To start understanding an existing business model, ask two questions:

1. **Who is the Customer?**
2. **What job does the Customer need to have done?**

To illuminate this idea, let's look at three enterprises.

First: Think about Jiffy Lube®, a drive-in, quick oil change service based in the United States. Few car owners are interested in changing engine oil themselves. Most lack the knowledge and tools — and prefer to avoid the preparation and potential mess of this dirty task (plus the hassle of recycling used oil). For $25 or $30, Jiffy Lube provides experts who let people do just that.

Next, consider Ning. Ning lets people easily and inexpensively make and manage customized social networks. Few companies (or individuals) have the money or expertise to build, host, and operate a social network that offers Facebook-like functionality. Enter Ning, which provides a simple, affordable substitute: a social network template, modifiable on multiple levels.

Finally, there's Vesta, a firm that completes electronic purchases on behalf of companies that serve hundreds of thousands of Customers daily. Handling high volumes of such transactions is complex and demands robust, leading-edge security and anti-fraud measures — two things that few companies can afford to develop and maintain in-house.

So, what do these three businesses have in common?
All receive payment for helping Customers get jobs done.

- Jiffy Lube performs crucial maintenance tasks (while keeping garages tidy and clothes clean) for vehicle owners.
- Ning's Customers are people who need to promote a cause; the company helps them build a community to do just that — at low cost and without hiring a technical specialist.
- Vesta helps businesses focus on specialties unrelated to payment collection.

Sounds simple, right?

Well, unlike in these three examples, defining "Customers" and "jobs" in sectors such as education, healthcare, government, finance, technology, and law can be challenging.

A big part of business model thinking is helping you identify and describe both Customers and jobs. Specifically, you'll learn how you can help Customers accomplish the jobs they need to do. And in doing so, you'll discover how to earn more money and gain more satisfaction from your work.

Every Organization Has a Business Model

Since a business model is the logic by which an enterprise sustains itself financially, does this mean that only for-profit corporations have business models?

No.

Every enterprise has a business model.
This is true because nearly every modern enterprise, whether for-profit, nonprofit, government, or otherwise, needs money to carry out its work.

For example, imagine you work for the New York Road Runners (NYRR), a nonprofit organization that promotes community health and fitness by holding running races, classes, clinics, and camps. Though NYRR is a nonprofit group, it must still:

- Pay staff salaries
- Purchase permits, pay utility, maintenance, legal, and other expenses
- Buy event supplies such as timing systems, bib numbers, refreshments, and finisher shirts and medals for its races
- Build a reserve fund for expanding services in the future

NYRR's main motivation is not financial gain; instead, its goal is to serve community "Customers" who want to stay fit. Still, even a nonprofit organization needs cash to carry out its work.

Therefore, like any other enterprise, NYRR *must be paid for helping Customers get jobs done.*

Let's ask our two business model questions about NYRR:

Who is the Customer?
NYRR's main Customers are runners and other community members who want support and camaraderie in their quest to maintain or improve fitness.

They include both annual members — people who pay to be part of the group and receive certain benefits as a result — and people who aren't annual members but who pay to participate in specific races and other events.

What job does the Customer need to have done?
NYRR's main job is hosting running-related events in the New York area.

NYRR is therefore a nonprofit group *whose Customers pay for its services.*

But what about organizations that provide free services to Customers? Does the business model idea still apply to them?

Yes!

Imagine a nonprofit group we'll call OrphanWatch, a charitable organization that houses, feeds, and teaches orphaned children. Like NYRR, Orphan-Watch needs cash to carry out its work. For example, it must:

- Buy food, clothes, books, and supplies for the children under its care
- Pay staff salaries
- Rent dormitory/school facilities, pay utility, maintenance, legal, and other expenses
- Build a reserve fund for expanding services in the future, etc.

Let's return again to our business model questions. In OrphanWatch's case, the answers are a bit different.

Who is the Customer?
OrphanWatch has two sets of Customers:
(1) children, who are the actual beneficiaries of the services, and (2) donors and other supporters who, by contributing money and purchasing crafts made by the children, enable OrphanWatch to accomplish its work.

What job does the Customer need to have done?
OrphanWatch has two jobs: (1) caring for orphaned children and (2) providing larger charitable organizations and individual donors with ways to fulfill their philanthropic duties and/or aspirations. In return for these opportunities, such Customers "pay" OrphanWatch in the form of gifts, grants, subscriptions, and product purchases.

Here's a key point: *Any organization that provides a free service to one Customer group must also have another set of Customers who subsidize those who don't pay.*

So you can see that our two business model questions *do* apply to OrphanWatch — just as they apply to any for-profit venture.

The Harsh Truth

What would happen to OrphanWatch if it stopped receiving donations and grants?

It would become unable to carry out its mission. Even if OrphanWatch's entire staff agreed to continue working without pay, the organization would be unable to cover other essential costs. Its only choice would be to shut down.

Nearly all enterprises operating in the modern economy (including governments!) face a harsh truth: *When cash runs out, the game's over.*

Different enterprises have different purposes. But to survive and thrive, all must abide by the logic of earning a livelihood. All must have a viable business model.

The definition of "viable" is simple: *More cash must come in than goes out.* Or, at the very least, *as much cash must come in as goes out.*

You've learned the basics about business models — how Customers and cash sustain enterprises. But business models involve more than just cash and Customers. The Business Model Canvas, which describes how nine components of a business model fit together, is a powerful technique for painting pictures of how organizations work.

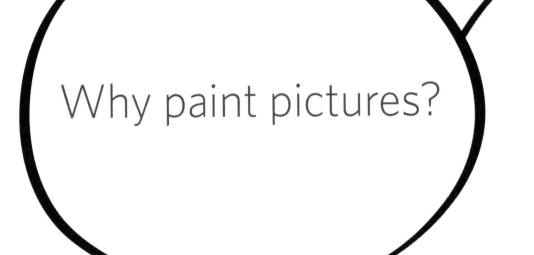

Why paint pictures?

Understanding how organizations work is no easy task. Large or complex organizations have so many components that it's tough to capture the big picture without visually depicting the enterprise.

Pictures also help turn unspoken assumptions into explicit information. And explicit information helps us think and communicate more effectively.

The Business Model Canvas provides a visual shorthand for simplifying complex organizations.

The Nine Building Blocks

The logic of how organizations provide Value to Customers

*Customers**

An organization serves
Customers . . .

*Value Provided**

. . . by solving Customer
problems or satisfying
Customer needs.

Channels

Organizations communicate
and deliver Value in different
ways . . .

Customer Relationships

. . . and establish and maintain
different kinds of relationships
with Customers.

*Revenue**

Money comes in
when Customers pay
for Value Provided.

Key Resources

These are the assets needed
to create and/or deliver
the previously described
elements.

Key Activities

These are the actual tasks
and actions required to create
and deliver the previously
described elements.

Key Partners

Some activities are
outsourced, and some
resources are acquired
outside the organization.

*Costs**

These are expenses incurred
acquiring Key Resources,
performing Key Activities, and
working with Key Partners.

* *Business Model Generation*
defines these building blocks as
Customer Segments, Value Proposition,
Revenue Streams, and Cost Structure,
respectively.

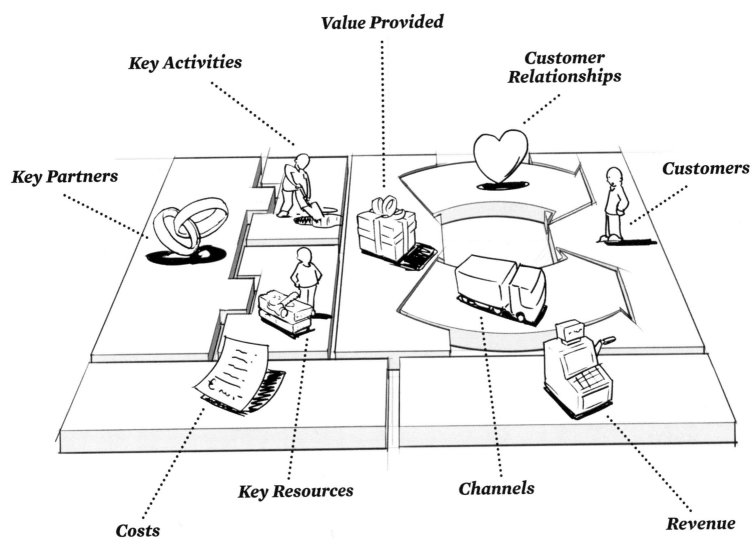

Key Activities

Value Provided

Customer Relationships

Key Partners

Customers

Key Resources

Channels

Costs

Revenue

Customers

Customers are the reason for an organization's existence.
No organization survives long without paying Customers.

Every organization serves one or more distinct Customer groups.

Organizations that serve other organizations are known as business-to-business
(b-to-b) enterprises. Organizations that serve consumers are known as business-
to-consumer (b-to-c) enterprises.

Some organizations serve both paying and non-paying Customers. Most Facebook
users, for example, pay Facebook nothing for its services. Yet without hundreds of
millions of non-paying Customers, Facebook would have nothing to sell to advertisers
or market researchers. Therefore, non-paying Customers may be essential to a
business model's success.

Things to remember about Customers:

- Different Customers may require different Value, Channels, or Relationships
- Some Customers pay, others may not
- Organizations often earn far more from one Customer group than from another

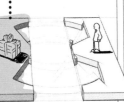

Value Provided

Think of Value Provided as Customer benefits created by "bundles" of services or products. The ability to provide exceptional Value is the key reason why Customers select one organization over another.

Here are examples of different elements of Value Provided:

Convenience
Saving Customers time or trouble is an important benefit. In the United States, for example, movie and game rental service Redbox places vending machines in frequently trafficked locations, such as supermarkets. For many users, Redbox provides the most convenient pickup/drop-off method of any movie rental service.

Price
Customers often choose a service because it saves them money. Skype, for example, provides international voice calling services at a better price than phone companies.

Design
Many Customers are willing to pay for excellent product and/or service design. Though more expensive than competitors, Apple's iPod is beautifully designed, both as a device and as part of an integrated music download/listening service.

Brand or status

Some companies provide Value by helping their Customers feel distinguished or prestigious. One illustration: People worldwide are willing to pay premium prices for Louis Vuitton luxury leather goods and fashions. That's because Louis Vuitton has shaped its brand to signify good taste, wealth, and appreciation of quality.

Cost reduction

Companies can help other enterprises reduce costs and, as a result, increase earnings. For example, instead of buying and continuously maintaining their own computer servers and advanced telecommunications infrastructure, more companies are finding it less costly to use third party-managed remote servers (cloud services) accessible via the Internet.

Risk reduction

Business Customers are also eager to reduce risk, particularly investment-related risk. Companies like Gartner, for instance, sell research and advisory services to help other companies predict the potential benefits of spending additional money on workplace technology.

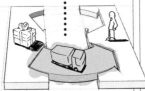

Channels

Channels perform five functions:

1. Create awareness of services or products
2. Help potential Customers *evaluate* products or services
3. Enable Customers to *purchase*
4. *Deliver* Value to Customers
5. *Ensure* post-purchase *satisfaction* through support

Typical channels include:

- In-person or telephone
- On-site or in-store
- Physical delivery
- The Internet (social media, blogs, e-mail, etc.)
- Traditional media (television, radio, newspapers, etc.)

Customer Relationships

Organizations must clearly define the type of relationship Customers prefer. Personal? Automated or self-service? Single transaction or subscription?

What's more, organizations should clarify the primary purpose of Customer Relationships. Is it to acquire new Customers? Retain existing Customers? Or derive more Revenue from existing Customers?

This purpose might change over time. For example, in the early days of mobile communications, cell phone companies focused on acquiring Customers, using aggressive tactics such as offering free phones. When the market matured, they changed their focus to retaining Customers and increasing average Revenue per Customer.

Here's another element to consider: More companies (like Amazon.com, YouTube, and Business Model You, LLC) are co-creating products or services with Customers.

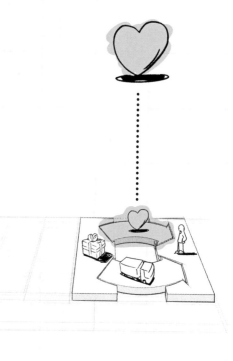

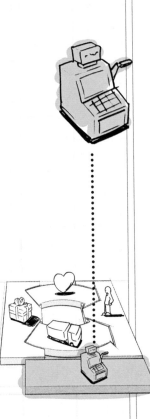

Revenue

Organizations must: (1) figure out what Value Customers are truly willing to pay for, and (2) accept payment in ways Customers prefer.

There are two categories of Revenue: (1) one-time Customer payments, and (2) recurring payments for products, services, or post-purchase maintenance or support. Here are some specific types:

Outright sale

This means Customers purchase ownership rights to a physical product. Toyota, for example, sells cars that buyers are free to drive, resell, dismantle, or destroy.

Lease or rent

Leasing means buying the temporary, exclusive right to use something for a fixed time, like a hotel room, apartment, or rental car. Those who rent or lease (lessees) avoid paying the full costs of ownership, while owners (lessors) enjoy recurring Revenue.

Service or usage fee

Telephone companies charge users by the minute, and delivery services charge Customers by the package. Doctors, lawyers, and other service providers charge by the hour or by the procedure. Advertising sellers like Google charge by the number of clickthroughs or exposures. Security services are paid to stand by and act when an alarm sounds.

Subscription fees

Magazines, gyms, and online game providers sell continuous access to services in the form of subscription fees.

Licensing

Intellectual property holders can give Customers permission to use their protected property in exchange for licensing fees.

Brokerage (matching) fees

Real estate firms like Century 21 earn brokerage fees by matching buyers with sellers, while job search services like Monster.com earn fees by matching job seekers with employers.

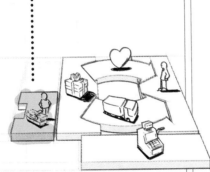

Key Resources

There are four types:

Human

All enterprises need people, but some business models depend especially heavily on human resources. The Mayo Clinic, for example, requires doctors and researchers with world-leading medical knowledge. Similarly, pharmaceutical manufacturers like Roche need top-notch scientists and many skilled salespeople.

Physical

Land, buildings, machines, and vehicles are crucial components of many business models. Amazon.com, for example, requires huge warehouses with massive conveyors and other expensive, specialized equipment.

Intellectual

Intellectual resources include intangibles such as brands, company-developed methods and systems, software, and patents or copyrights. Jiffy Lube® has a strong brand — as well as its own methods for serving Customers — that it licenses to franchisees. Telecommunications chipset designer Qualcomm built its business model around patented designs that earn licensing fees.

Financial

Financial resources include cash, lines of credit, or financial guarantees. Telecommunications equipment manufacturer Ericsson sometimes borrows from banks, then uses a portion of the proceeds to help Customers finance equipment purchases, ensuring that orders are placed with Ericsson rather than competitors.

Key Activities

These are the most important things an organization
must do to make its business model work.

Making includes manufacturing products, designing/developing/delivering
services, and solving problems. For service companies, "making" can mean both
preparing to deliver services in the future and delivering those services. This is
because services, such as getting a haircut, are "consumed" as they are delivered.

Selling means promoting, advertising, or educating potential Customers about
service or product Value. Specific tasks might include making sales calls, planning
or executing advertisements or promotions, and educating or training.

Supporting helps keep the entire organization running smoothly but isn't directly
associated with either making or selling. Examples include hiring people and doing
bookkeeping or other administrative work.

We tend to think of our work in terms of tasks — Key Activities — rather than in
terms of the *Value* those activities provide. But when Customers choose an organization, they're more interested in the *Value* they'll receive than in the task itself.

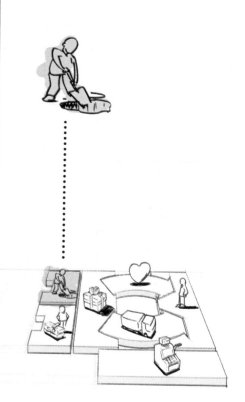

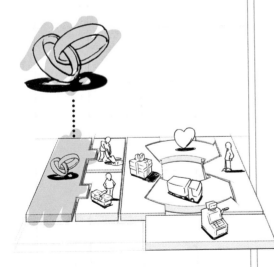

Key Partners

This network helps make a business model effective.

It would be illogical for an organization to own every resource or perform every activity by itself. Some activities require expensive equipment or exceptional expertise. That's why most organizations outsource payroll preparation to companies like Paychex that specialize in such work.

Partnerships, though, can go beyond "make" and "buy" relationships. A wedding gown rental firm, a florist, and a photographer, for example, might share their Customer lists with each other at no cost to collaborate on promotional activities that benefit all three parties.

Costs

Acquiring Key Resources, performing Key Activities,
and working with Key Partnerships all incur Costs.

Cash is needed to create and deliver Value, maintain Customer Relationships, and generate Revenue. Costs can be roughly calculated after defining Key Resources, Key Activities, and Key Partners.

"Scalability" is an important concept related to both Cost and to a business model's overall effectiveness. Being scalable means a business can effectively deal with big increases in demand — it has the capacity to effectively serve many more Customers without straining or sacrificing quality. In financial terms, being scalable means the extra cost of serving each additional Customer falls instead of remaining constant or rising.

A software company is a good example of a scalable business. Once developed, a software program can be reproduced and distributed at low cost. The expense of serving an additional Customer who downloads a program, for instance, is essentially zero.

In contrast, consulting businesses and personal service firms are rarely scalable. That's because each hour spent serving an additional Customer requires another hour of practitioner time — the extra cost of serving each additional Customer remains constant. From a financial viewpoint, therefore, scalable businesses are more attractive than non-scalable businesses.

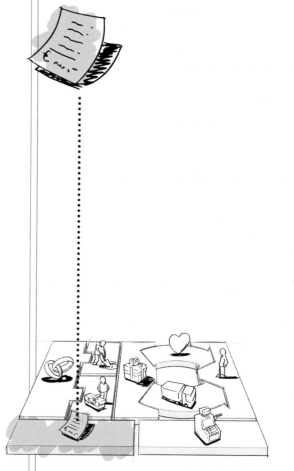

Drawings by JAM

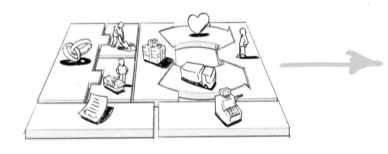

Together the nine building blocks form

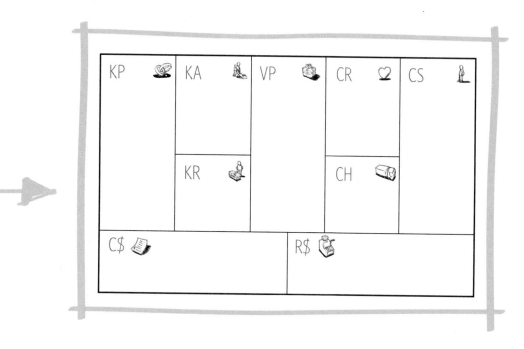

a useful tool: the Business Model Canvas.

Now It's Your Turn

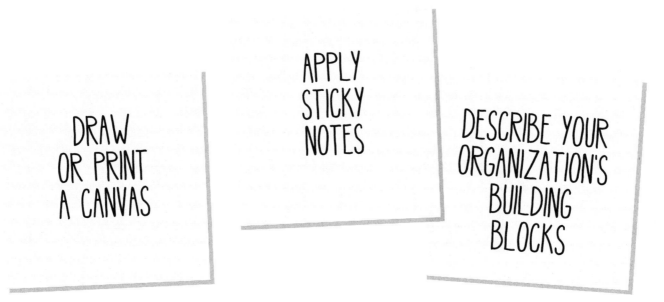

My Organization's Business Model

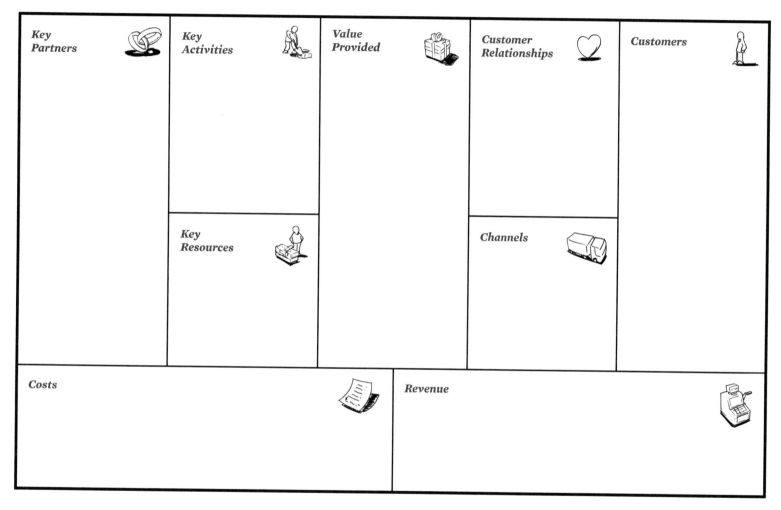

Key Partners	Key Activities	Value Provided	Customer Relationships	Customers
	Key Resources		Channels	

Costs

Revenue

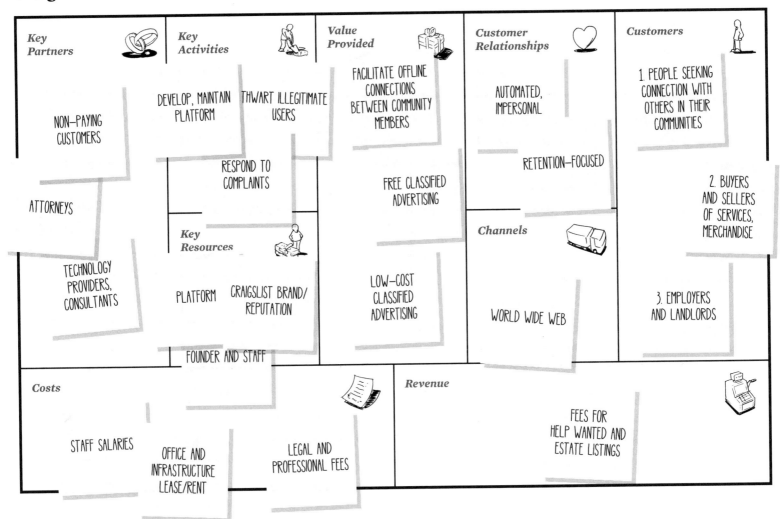

craigslist's Business Model

Key Partners

NON–PAYING CUSTOMERS

ATTORNEYS

TECHNOLOGY PROVIDERS, CONSULTANTS

Key Activities

DEVELOP, MAINTAIN PLATFORM

THWART ILLEGITIMATE USERS

RESPOND TO COMPLAINTS

Key Resources

PLATFORM

CRAIGSLIST BRAND/ REPUTATION

FOUNDER AND STAFF

Value Provided

FACILITATE OFFLINE CONNECTIONS BETWEEN COMMUNITY MEMBERS

FREE CLASSIFIED ADVERTISING

LOW–COST CLASSIFIED ADVERTISING

Customer Relationships

AUTOMATED, IMPERSONAL

RETENTION–FOCUSED

Channels

WORLD WIDE WEB

Customers

1. PEOPLE SEEKING CONNECTION WITH OTHERS IN THEIR COMMUNITIES

2. BUYERS AND SELLERS OF SERVICES, MERCHANDISE

3. EMPLOYERS AND LANDLORDS

Costs

STAFF SALARIES

OFFICE AND INFRASTRUCTURE LEASE/RENT

LEGAL AND PROFESSIONAL FEES

Revenue

FEES FOR HELP WANTED AND ESTATE LISTINGS

Craigslist offers classified advertising to help people find jobs and housing, connect with community members, and buy, sell, or barter services and merchandise. The company hosts 700 sites in 70 countries and posts more than one million job listings each month. Despite its non-corporate culture, craigslist is one of the world's most profitable firms on an earnings-per-employee basis: Its staff of 30 generates annual sales exceeding $100 million, say industry analysts.[4]

Customers

Most craigslist Customers pay nothing for the service. Craigslist charges listing fees to employers and landlords in some cities. These paying customers subsidize non-paying Customers.

Value Provided

As an online service, craigslist is unusual in providing Value by facilitating *offline* connections between community members. Another Value it provides is free classified advertising, which Customers employ for nearly every service and product imaginable. Providing these Values has generated a massive, devoted Customer base that lets craigslist offer a third Value: effective, low-cost advertisements for employers and landlords.

Channels

The service is promoted and delivered exclusively through the Internet.

Customer Relationships

Users create, edit, and post listings on the craigslist site using an automated process that eliminates the need for intervention by craigslist staff. Staff rely primarily on users to moderate forums and identify fraudulent activity. Craigslist concentrates on optimizing the user experience for current Customers rather than innovating to attract new Customers.

Revenue

Only employers and landlords (Customer group 3) generate Revenue for craigslist.

Key Resources

Craigslist's number one resource is its "platform." A platform is an automated mechanism or "engine" that enables interactions between Customers. Craigslist founder Craig Newmark's reputation and public service philosophy is another key resource, as are the site's general manager and staff.

Key Activities

Craigslist's most important activity is developing and maintaining its platform. Think of it this way: Google could lose 100 engineers tomorrow without missing a beat, but having its Web site go down for a day would be a catastrophe. In relative terms, the same is true for craigslist. Aside from platform development and maintenance, staff spend time dealing with hackers, spammers, and other illegitimate users.

Key Partners

Non-paying Customers are craigslist's most important Partners, because they strive to maintain honesty and civility among users.

Costs

As a privately held company, craigslist is not obligated to disclose Revenues or earnings. But it operates out of modest offices with a staff of 30, so its Costs are tiny compared to other online giants such as Facebook, Twitter, and eBay. Key recurring expenses include salaries, server and telecommunications infrastructure fees, and office rent. Its stature within the industry and many side projects mean craigslist also incurs substantial legal and professional fees. In fact, some observers believe these expenses exceed all other Costs combined.

CHAPTER 3
The Personal Business Model Canvas

Now, let's focus on the most important business model of all: business model <u>you</u>.

The Canvas works for describing personal business models just as it does for describing organizational business models. Note a couple of differences between the two, though:

- In a personal business model, the Key Resource is you: your interests, skills and abilities, personality, and the assets you own or control. In organizations, Key Resources often include a broader range of resources, such as other people.

- A personal business model takes into account unquantifiable "soft" Costs (such as stress) and "soft" Benefits (such as satisfaction). The organizational business model generally considers only monetary Costs and Benefits.

When drawing a personal business model, you may find these alternative building block descriptions helpful:

PERSONAL
The Business Model Canvas

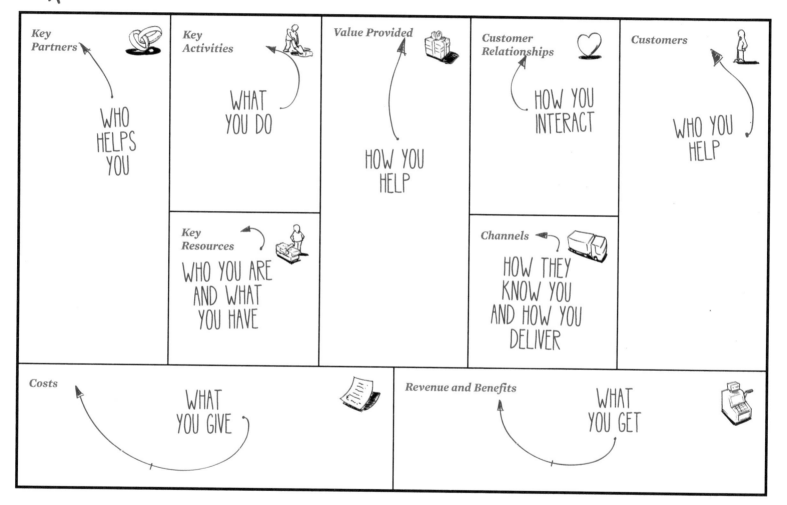

Key Partners

WHO HELPS YOU

Key Activities

WHAT YOU DO

Key Resources

WHO YOU ARE AND WHAT YOU HAVE

Value Provided

HOW YOU HELP

Customer Relationships

HOW YOU INTERACT

Channels

HOW THEY KNOW YOU AND HOW YOU DELIVER

Customers

WHO YOU HELP

Costs

WHAT YOU GIVE

Revenue and Benefits

WHAT YOU GET

To download a PDF of the personal Business Model Canvas, visit **BusinessModelYou.com**.

Your First Personal Business Model: Drafting time!

Grab paper, pencil, and sticky notes; this chapter is where your personal business model begins to take shape. A few things to keep in mind: While drafting your first personal business model, limit yourself to the professional work you do to earn a living.

Painting a clear, accurate picture of your professional activities lays the foundation for later addressing "soft" career elements such as satisfaction, stress, recognition, time demands, social contribution, etc.

THESE REINVENTORS WILL HELP YOU WITH EACH BUILDING BLOCK

A Personal Story for Every Building Block

Who helps you
(Key Partners)

What you do
(Key Activities)

How you help
(Value Provided)

How you interact
(Customer Relationships)

Who you help
(Customers)

Who you are and what you have
(K...)

**How they know you and how you deliver (Ch...)*

**What you give (C...)*

What you get (Reven... ...nefits)

Key Resources
(Who You Are/What You Have)

Organizations can attract significant human, financial, physical, and intellectual resources: people, money, equipment, real estate, and intellectual property. Individuals, though, are "resource constrained" — we must rely primarily on ourselves. Your personal Key Resources include *who you are*: (1) your interests, (2) abilities and skills, and (3) personality, and *what you have*: knowledge, experience, personal and professional contacts, and other tangible and intangible resources or assets.

Your interests — the things that excite you — may well be your most precious resource. That's because interests drive career satisfaction. **List your strongest interests in the Key Resources building block.**

Abilities and skills are next. Abilities are natural, innate talents: things you do easily or effortlessly. **List specifics** such as *spatial reasoning, group facilitation, mechanical aptitude*. Skills, on the other hand, are learned or acquired talents: things you've gotten better at through practice and study. **List specifics** such as *nursing, financial analysis, building construction, computer programming*.

Personality completes *who you are* (at least for now). **Write down some descriptors**, such as *good emotional intelligence, industrious, outgoing, calm, poised, thoughtful, energetic, detail-oriented*, etc.

Naturally, who you are encompasses more than interests, abilities and skills, and personality: It includes values, intellect, sense of humor, education, purpose, and much more. For now, though, let's move on to *what you have*. What you have includes tangible and intangible assets. If you enjoy an extensive network of professional contacts, for example, **jot down** *extensive network*. Similarly, **you might list** deep industry experience, strong professional reputation, thought leadership in a specific field, or any publications or other intellectual property to your credit.

Finally, write down any personally owned tangible assets that are essential or potentially useful to your work, such as vehicles, tools, special clothing, money or physical assets available to invest in your career, and so forth.

PROFILE:

THE DOCTOR

Dr. Annabelle Slingerland specializes in pediatric diabetes treatment and research — and is a strong believer in empowering young patients too often told that life is full of limitations and dangers. To promote her beliefs, Annabelle organized an all-volunteer relay marathon for children with diabetes. She dubbed the event "Kids Chain."

Shortly before marathon day, tragedy struck: Annabelle was involved in a serious bicycle accident. The event took place and succeeded — attracting unexpectedly strong corporate, government, and media attention — but Annabelle became unable to continue her clinical practice as a physician. Her future seemed bleak.

Still, corporate and media interest in Kids Chain remained strong. "I didn't realize it was a potentially life-fulfilling project for me," she recalls. "I even tried to let go of it. But Kids Chain wouldn't let go of me."

Forum member Marieke Post showed Annabelle how to use the Canvas to design a nonprofit organization that could support Kids Chain. Annabelle experienced a flash of insight while examining her Key Resources building block. "I realized I should consider myself one of Kids Chain's most important resources, and that the organization should pay me for my input," she remembers. "I'd never thought of it like that before."

Today Annabelle serves as director of the nonprofit foundation Kids Chain for Diabetes.

Key Activities
(What You Do)

Key Activities — what you do — are driven by Key Resources. In other words, what you do evolves naturally out of who you are.

Start filling in this building block by thinking about the handful of critical tasks you perform regularly at work. Remember, Key Activities are simply physical or mental activities performed on behalf of Customers. They don't describe the more important Value created by performing such activities.

Even so, naming specific tasks is a straightforward way to continue painting your personal Business Model Canvas — and will prepare you to thoughtfully consider the more crucial idea of Value.

List those tasks now. Your work may involve only two or three Key Activities, or it may require half a dozen or more. On your Canvas, list only the truly important activities — the ones that distinguish your occupation from others — rather than every task you perform.

PROFILE:

THE ENGINEER

"Throughout my school years and early career, I focused intently on personal development —and wondered why the benefits never materialized. I graduated near the top of my class at the Naval Academy, got a master's degree in electrical engineering, served as a nuclear engineer in the Navy, and completed an MBA while working full-time. But despite these accomplishments, I felt stuck in jobs suited for the least common denominator. I felt like a commodity engineer.

"While looking for ways to increase my satisfaction, I discovered the personal business model. I painted my own Canvas, and almost immediately my problem became clear. Despite all my personal development efforts, I had neglected to figure out how my skills could help other people. When I tried to fill in the "What you do" and "Who you help" building blocks, I had almost nothing to write down.

"Making the transition from a skill focus to a value focus is agonizingly hard. That's why the personal business model idea is about more than the Canvas. It showed me that I had to find an interest I was passionate about—one that would satisfy me personally but help others at the same time.

"I can't shake my feelings about the evolving role of fathers. I'm still figuring out exactly how I can help. I'm confused personally about how to be an equal parent with my wife. What traditional mom-chores do I need to learn how to do? My hypothesis is that many other fathers are silently asking themselves the same questions. Now I'm working to create a business model that addresses the new, expanded role of the father as a nurturer."

Customers

(Who You Help)

Next, add Customers — who you help — to your Canvas. Recall that Customers are those who pay to receive a benefit (or who receive a benefit at no cost and are subsidized by paying Customers).

As an individual, your Customers or Customer groups include the people within your organization who depend on your help to get jobs done (if you are self-employed, you can consider your professional situation your organization).

Importantly, this includes your boss, supervisor, and others who are directly responsible for compensating you. They authorize the organization to pay you; therefore, they comprise one set of Customers.

So, if you have an immediate boss or supervisor, **write their name** in the Customer building block.

Who else do you report to? **Write these names** or roles in the Customer building block as well.

Now, step back a moment and think. What roles do you play at work? Do you serve others within your organization? Do you hand off work to colleagues?

Who depends on you or benefits from your work? These people may not pay you directly, but your overall job performance — and the reason you continue to get paid — depends on how well you serve particular colleagues.

For example, if you are part of a computer or technology support team, you know all too well what it means to have internal Customers! Are there other individuals or groups within the organization you might consider Customers? How about key project leaders or team members? If so, **jot down their name(s)**.

Next, think about other parties involved with your organization. How about Customers or companies who purchase or use your organization's services or products? Do you deal with them directly? Even if you don't, you might want to consider them your Customers.

Do you interact with any of your organization's Key Partners? Maybe they deserve a place on your Customer list.

Finally, consider the greater communities served by your work. Such communities might include neighborhoods or cities, or groups of people bound by common commercial, professional, or social interests.

CASE STUDY:
CUSTOMERS

NOTES:

REWRITING THE CUSTOMER STORY

NAME

TRINA BOWERMAN

PROFILE:
THE WEDDING PHOTOGRAPHER

Trina Bowerman attended a personal business model workshop, and after the session, approached the facilitator. She said she loved the ideas presented, but she didn't see how to apply the personal business model methodology to her own situation.

"What kind of work do you do?" the facilitator asked.

"I'm a wedding photographer," she replied.

"So you tell wedding stories with photographs," the facilitator observed.

"Well, in a way . . . yes."

"So why not try telling stories about events other than weddings?"

Trina's hands dropped to her sides, and she rocked back on her heels.
"Thank you," she said a moment later. "Now I'll have trouble sleeping tonight."

63

Value Provided
(How You Help)

Now it's time to define the Value you provide to Customers: how you help other people get their jobs done. As noted earlier, this is the most important concept for thinking about your career.

A good way to begin defining Value is to ask yourself, "What job is the Customer 'hiring' me to perform? What benefits do Customers gain as a result of that job?"

For example, earlier we saw that the Value Jiffy Lube provides to Customers lies not in the physical act of changing oil, but in the advantages people gain by getting help from professionals: trouble-free cars, no mess, less hassle.

Understanding how your Key Activities result in Value Provided to Customers is central to defining your personal business model.

PROFILE:

THE TRANSLATOR

Mika Uchigasaki is a full-time translator working between English and Japanese. Law firms are among her most important Customers.

She attended a personal business model workshop at a translators' conference. During the session, the facilitator commented on Mika's first-ever, in-progress Canvas.

In her Value Provided building block, Mika had written "translate documents from Japanese to English."

"How does translating documents from Japanese to English differ from Key Activities?" the facilitator asked.

Mika looked puzzled.

"What job is the law firm hiring you to help them with?" the facilitator continued.

Mika thought for a moment. "Win a lawsuit," she replied.

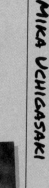

"So help them do that job," the facilitator went on. "'Translating documents from Japanese to English' is a Key Activity. Your Value Provided might be something like 'creating persuasive documentation to help win a multi-million dollar lawsuit.' Never let clients equate Key Activities with Value Provided."

Mika's eyes shone. "This is a new way of thinking for me," she said. "I've been searching for a way to remodel my work. I think I've found it."

When you can clearly define Customers and Value Provided, you've completed much of the work needed to draw a personal business model. Now for the rest:

Channels
(How They Know You/ How You Deliver)

This building block encompasses five phases of what's known in business jargon as "the marketing process." The phases are best described in question form:

1. How will potential Customers discover how you can help them?
2. How will they decide whether to buy your service?
3. How will they buy it?
4. How will you deliver what Customers buy?
5. How will you follow-up to make sure Customers are happy?

Defining the Channels through which you deliver what Customers buy is straightforward: You may submit written reports; talk to people; upload code to a development server; deliver oral presentations in person or online; or use vehicles to physically deliver merchandise.

But as the five-phase process shows, there are other more interesting and more important Channel phases, including *how potential Customers get to know you and your Value Provided.*

Will they learn about you through word-of-mouth? A Web site or blog? Articles or speaking engagements? Sales calls? E-mail messages or online forums? Advertisements?

Here's a powerful reminder of why Channels are crucial to your personal business model: (1) You must *define* how you help to *communicate* how you help, (2) you must *communicate* how you help to *sell* how you help, and (3) you must *sell* how you help in order to *get paid* for helping.

CASE STUDY:
CHANNELS

NOTES:
CHANGING CHANNELS

PROFILE:

THE FREELANCE GRAPHIC DESIGNER

"I'm easily bored. After starting work as a graphic designer, I moved from job to job, rarely staying long in one position. The small companies I worked for didn't appreciate my lack of patience for details or my efforts to stay interested by fiddling with the workflow. Often I was fired after a couple of months; sometimes I left to pursue another opportunity. With no entrepreneurial background, I didn't realize that I was the perfect freelancer until one of my employers mentioned it — right after firing me.

"I knew nothing about business models or Value-based personal marketing. But aside from my design skills, two of my strengths are that I love meeting new people and taking on several new projects at once.

"For example, it was easy for me to walk into an advertising agency's graphic design department for the first time and get acquainted quickly. By lunchtime everybody thought I had worked there for years, because I knew the people, their clients, and the department processes.

"Being easily bored and constantly wanting to meet new people and tackle new projects can work against you when you're a full-time employee. But when I changed my Channel from employee to freelancer, these qualities became key strengths. My colleagues had the same or even better technical skills. But because it only took me an hour to become familiar with a new setting, I found myself in high demand."

NAME

KEN TIMMERMAN

65

Customer Relationships
(How You Interact)

How would you describe the way you interact with Customers? Do you provide personal, face-to-face service? Or are your relationships more "hands off," relying primarily on e-mail or other written communications? Are your relationships characterized by single transactions or by ongoing services? Do you focus on growing your Customer base (acquisition) or on satisfying existing Customers (retention)? **Note your answers on your Canvas.**

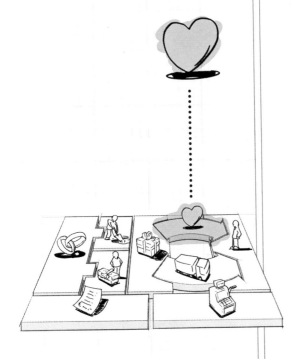

CASE STUDY:
CUSTOMER RELATIONSHIPS

NOTES:
CONNECT ON THEIR TERMS

PROFILE:

THE ACCOUNT MANAGER

Jessica Ho started a sales job for an office and paper products manufacturer and was assigned major U.S. accounts including Staples and Office Max. But after several months, she was still struggling to develop good relationships with her Customers. So she sought help from Jim Wylie, a business coach recommended by her boss.

Wylie focused first on Jessica's Customer Relationships building block. He found she had a very pleasant demeanor and was a strong verbal communicator. But aside from visiting clients to take or deliver orders, she rarely called them. Jessica admitted she was "a child of the digital age" who felt more comfortable sending e-mail than speaking in person or by phone.

Wylie suggested that Jessica use her cell phone to call clients whenever the opportunity arose. Jessica followed the advice, and soon she was enjoying warmer relationships with her clients. Calling by phone often made things happen more quickly and created rapport that carried over to in-person meetings.

69

Key Partners
(Who Helps You)

Your Key Partners are those who support you as a professional — and help you do your job successfully. Key Partners may provide motivation, advice, or opportunities for growth. They may also give you other resources needed to complete certain tasks well. Partners may include colleagues or mentors at work, members of your professional network, family or friends, or professional advisers. **List any Key Partners now.** Later, you may choose to broaden your definition of Key Partners.

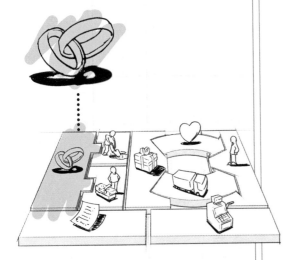

PROFILE:

THE SALES PROFESSIONAL

Jon Taylor was a sales representative with 20 years of experience selling raw materials to plastics industry Customers. He had always enjoyed freedom in managing clients; he was able to set his own price and payment terms, and he submitted little internal documentation on his sales activities. That all changed when Jon's company was acquired by a large international company.

Within the new, larger organization, Jon discovered that his style irritated "inside" staff members who provided salespeople with administrative and marketing support. These staff members gave salespeople price and term guidelines, and requested activity documentation so they could monitor sales actions and report to management.

Revisiting his personal business model, Jon realized that the acquisition had brought him a new set of internal Key Partners who were nearly as important as his outside Customers to his personal success. He also recognized that his "hands-off" style was outdated.

Jon decided to start submitting activity documentation to his new internal Partners and calling the sales manager and internal support staff frequently. These simple new behaviors wowed — and won over — his colleagues.

71

Revenues and Benefits

(What You Get)

Write down income sources, such as salary, contractor or professional fees, stock options, royalties, and any other cash payments. Add benefits such as health insurance, retirement packages, or tuition assistance. Later, when you reflect on how you want to modify your personal business model, you can take into account "soft" benefits, such as increased satisfaction, recognition, and social contribution.

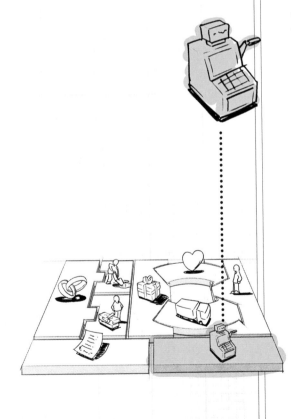

PROFILE:

THE EXECUTIVE ASSISTANT

Jet Barendregt was an executive assistant to a senior partner at a European branch of accounting consultancy PricewaterhouseCoopers LLP (PwC).

As PwC's business grew, the firm added positions comparable to Jet's. But turnover was high, and Jet found herself coaching new recruits, even while shouldering additional, heavier responsibilities. After ten years, Jet had become indispensable to the firm — but felt her expertise and Value were taken for granted.

So when her employer announced a location change that would dramatically lengthen her commute, Jet decided it was time to reinvent her personal business model.

She left PwC and set up a virtual personal assistant service, serving clients entirely through e-mail, telephone, Skype, and cloud-based tools. Her key innovation was in the Revenue and Benefits building block: She replaced her salary with a monthly subscription fee.

Today, Jet is commute-free, has more time for her children and other interests, and earns three times what she did at PwC. What's more, she's able to choose her clients. "My experience shows you can actually increase Revenue and Benefits while lowering Costs," Jet says. "All it takes is commitment, trust — and the right model."

Costs
(What You Give)

Costs are what you give to your work: time, energy, and money, mostly.

List any unreimbursed hard costs, such as:

- Training or subscription fees
- Commuting, travel, or socializing expenses
- Vehicles, tools, or special clothing
- Internet, telephone, transportation, or utility expenses you bear while working at home or at client sites

Costs also include stress or dissatisfaction brought on by Key Activities or working with Key Partners. We'll discuss such "soft" costs in the next chapter.

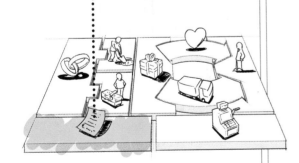

PROFILE:

THE ADVERTISING EXECUTIVE

"When Mark Degginger walked into my office, it was like neon signs were telling me that he had the wrong job," says career counselor Fran Moga. "He was miserable. He had a six-figure salary, a beautiful house, and a sweet boat. But he had to drag himself to work each day. He took long lunches just so he could tolerate afternoons.

"He worked for a very earnings-driven advertising agency; it was high-stress and dog-eat-dog. He also had a bad back — he was younger than me, but he looked older.

"The biggest problem was that though he was competent, work caused a conflict of values. He had all the trappings of success, but wanted something that would give him a sense of contributing to the greater good.

"So one day I asked, 'Why do you keep doing this? Have you ever thought about what it's costing you?' He left without a word. But at the next session, he seemed to understand. 'I'm paying a price in relationships, health, and enjoyment of life,' he said.

"When Mark arrived at one of our last meetings, I knew things were better even before he spoke. He appeared brighter and more relaxed.

"'How are you?' I asked. 'I'm great!' he said. He'd resigned from his ad agency job, and he and his wife had agreed to downsize. He had taken a position with a nonprofit corporation that trains disadvantaged and disabled people. It was a big cut in salary. But he was much happier."

KEY POINT:

CUSTOMERS OWN JOBS

PROFILE:

THE DOCTORAL STUDENT

A journalist by training and experience, Chris Burns watched as traditional publishing industry business models — including her own employer's — withered before the Internet onslaught. By the time she was laid off, she had enrolled in a doctoral program with the goal of becoming a writing professor.

Thanks to her strong interest in sustainability issues and connections provided by her doctoral committee members, Chris found part-time work copyediting scholarly papers for university professors. To her surprise, she enjoyed this work.

One day, Chris realized her *real* job wasn't copyediting, it was something far more valuable: helping Customers get articles published in leading scholarly journals. So she decided to raise her hourly rate significantly and charge for research time.

The result? She won more Customers than ever.

In retrospect, Chris recognized two common flaws in her initial model:

Equating Key Activities with Value

Instead of identifying the Customer job-to-be-done at the highest level — and defining Value in terms of that job — Chris equated Value Provided with her editing and rewriting activities. This diminished her offer's worth.

Owning the job

Chris "owned" the job from the start. That left her work narrowly defined by Customers as "improving readability and style." When she started reminding Customers that getting published was *their* job — and one she could help with — her Value (and reputation) soared.

How Chris Revised Her Personal Business Model

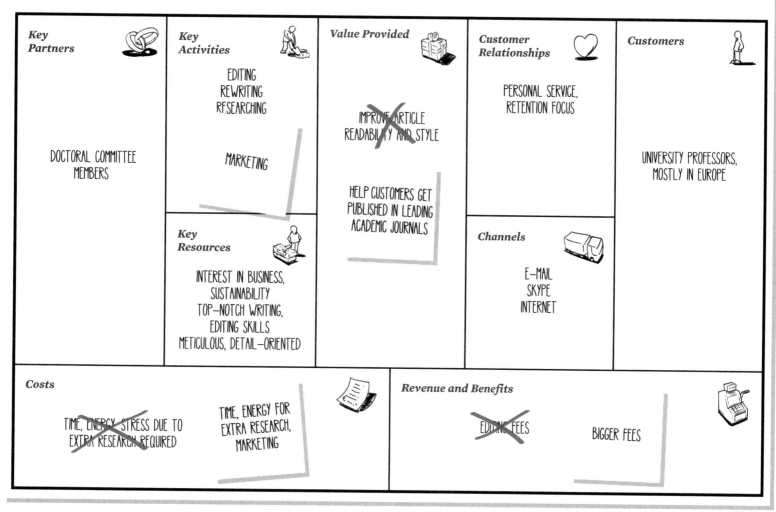

Key Partners

DOCTORAL COMMITTEE MEMBERS

Key Activities

EDITING
REWRITING
RESEARCHING

MARKETING

Key Resources

INTEREST IN BUSINESS, SUSTAINABILITY
TOP-NOTCH WRITING, EDITING SKILLS
METICULOUS, DETAIL-ORIENTED

Value Provided

~~IMPROVE ARTICLE READABILITY AND STYLE~~

HELP CUSTOMERS GET PUBLISHED IN LEADING ACADEMIC JOURNALS

Customer Relationships

PERSONAL SERVICE, RETENTION FOCUS

Channels

E-MAIL
SKYPE
INTERNET

Customers

UNIVERSITY PROFESSORS, MOSTLY IN EUROPE

Costs

~~TIME, ENERGY STRESS DUE TO EXTRA RESEARCH REQUIRED~~

TIME, ENERGY FOR EXTRA RESEARCH, MARKETING

Revenue and Benefits

~~EDITING FEES~~

BIGGER FEES

Reflect

Revisit your life direction and consider how you want to align your personal and career aspirations.

CHAPTER 4
Who Are You?

PUTTING WHO YOU ARE INTO WHAT YOU DO

THE DOG RUNNER

When Andrea Wellman was laid off her commercial photography job, she tried to avoid panicking. She didn't rush to the nearest temporary help agency, apply for customer service positions on craigslist, or hit up family for quick cash.

Instead, she filled her suddenly empty schedule with appointments she'd missed while working: appointments with herself.

Andrea admits the temptation to grab a part-time job "just to bring in some money" was strong. Fortunately, her need for personal reflection — and a new personal business model — won out. "Until I lost my job," she says, "I'd been operating on autopilot. I thought this might be my best opportunity to find how to regain some control over my career."

Andrea's crazy about two things: dogs and running. Born in the shadow of a Saint Bernard, she's never been without a canine friend. And although she took up running later, she loves a good five-miler — or a good marathon — as much as she loves her pets. In fact, a few months before she was laid off from her photography job, Andrea had combined her two passions: She'd started running her puppy, Molly. Occasionally, she'd pick up a friend's dog too, and the three would trot through the friendly Seattle streets.

After Andrea lost her job, she kept running Molly. And because she had more time, she started running other dogs on behalf of friends. "It kept me sane," she says. "Not just that, but it kept me happy — I felt unworried, even ecstatic, while running with the pups."

One day while flipping through an issue of *Runner's World* magazine, Andrea read a career-changing story. "There was a guy in Chicago who runs dogs full-time," she remembers. "It was all he did!" At first, Andrea was skeptical anyone could make a living running pets. But she looked him up. Sure enough, he was a full-time professional dog runner.

Andrea immediately called her friends. She told them about the Chicago dog runner and asked whether they'd pay her to keep running with their dogs. To her surprise, they agreed. "They said they'd seen positive changes in their dogs since I'd started running them," she recollects. "My friends believed the runs were helping their pets' well-being — so they were happy to pay."

Andrea was elated.

At first, her new income was a helpful trickle rather than a bona fide cashflow. But friends were so pleased with the service that they talked about it: with other friends, at work, out on the town. And suddenly, strangers started seeking Andrea's services. She was thrilled. "I honestly didn't think of it as a 'real' job," she says. "I always agreed to add another dog, but it was because I loved doing it and saw how much the dogs loved it too."

People kept inquiring, and eventually Andrea realized she could pay rent with her dog-running income. A few months later, she was able to pay more of her expenses. One day, Andrea realized that what had begun as a pastime had gradually become her profession — meaning she had to start thinking in business terms. She added pet insurance. She got certified in pet CPR. She made a Web site.

Today, Andrea can make a full-time living as a dog runner. She has more than 50 clients — so many that she's hired other runners to help. As she sees it, that's a big part of what makes her business worthwhile. "My work's become more than *me* living *my* dream," she says. "I've created a way for other runners to live theirs — and to me that's incredibly satisfying."

Dream jobs are more often *created* than *found*, so they're rarely attainable through conventional searches. Creating one requires strong self-knowledge.

MY DREAM JOB:

Discovering You

"Most job-hunters who fail to find their dream job fail not because they lack information about the *job market*, but because they lack information about *themselves*," says Dick Bolles, author of *What Color is Your Parachute?*, the English-language career guide that's been a top-seller for the past 40 years.[5] Dream jobs are more often *created* than *found*, so they're rarely attainable through conventional searches. Creating one requires strong self-knowledge.

As in Andrea's case, though, it often takes a crisis — such as losing a job or failing at a new business — for us to reflect carefully on our careers and ourselves. Without one, extensive self-reflection may strike us as selfish. But thinking about yourself is *not* selfish, says Bolles, because it is concerned with what *the world most needs* from you.

What's more, reflecting deeply on who you are before crisis strikes rewards both you and your Customers because it helps prevent burnout and disillusionment. When you're personally satisfied, you're more able to help others.

But without impending trouble pushing us, how can we dive into meaningful self-reflection?

The World Beyond Work

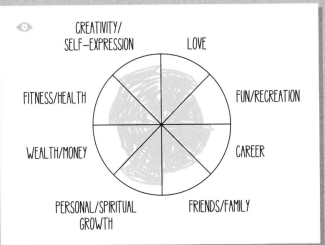

Career professionals sometimes have clients start this self-reflection process with the Wheel of Life. There are different versions of the Wheel, but each shows a number of broad themes or interest areas, such as Fitness/Health, Career, Wealth/Money, Personal/Spiritual Growth, Fun/Recreation, Love, Friends/Family, Physical Environment/Home, Creativity/Self-Expression, and Lifestyle/Possessions.

The idea is to choose eight themes you find most relevant, and assign one theme to each segment of the Wheel.

To do the Wheel of Life exercise

- Choose eight of the themes listed above (or mix and match with your own themes/interest areas).
- On a separate sheet of paper or using the blank Wheel on page 87, plot your level of satisfaction with each category by marking points along the segment spokes — considering the Wheel's center "zero satisfaction" and the perimeter "complete satisfaction."
- Once you have finished, connect your points and shade in the center area.

A completely shaded circle would represent total fulfillment in every aspect of life. A partially shaded circle, such as the one above, reveals life elements that may need more attention.

Career counselors sometimes have clients complete the exercise, then take a different-colored pencil and shade in additional areas representing where they'd *like* to be within each segment. They remind clients that not everyone prioritizes things the same way: A segment that's 50 percent shaded on Friends/Family, for instance, may be adequate for one person and unacceptably low for another.

The Wheel of Life exercise provides clues to the broad themes within which our core interests lie. At the same time, it reminds us of dimensions of life that may be as important as work — or even more important.

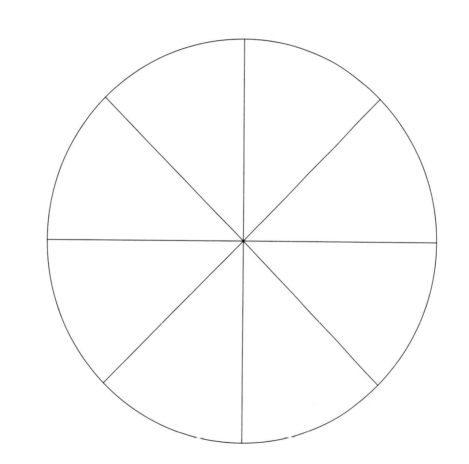

Answering the "Who Am I?" Question

After thinking about where work and other current pursuits fit in your life, maybe you've noticed some imbalance. How can you restore equilibrium?

Remember how Andrea found increased satisfaction and purpose? She returned to things she'd long loved. And as it turns out, the things we enjoyed as children can illuminate our paths as adults.

As children, we knew who we were and what we liked to do, even if we lacked the vocabulary to explain ourselves.

But, as Marcus Buckingham puts it, at some point, "Your childish clarity faded, and you started listening to the world around you more closely than you did to yourself. The world was persuasive and loud, and so you resigned yourself to conforming to its demands."[6]

It's worth considering the possibility that our careers and values evolved around expectations set by others rather than by us. Especially with respect to career decisions, family, peers, and teachers often urge us to make choices based on "security," "stability," "respectability," "good pay," or other attributes.

One problem with others' expectations, though, is that we might adopt them as our own; a desire for social acceptance can easily overwhelm our internal compasses.

But what if others' expectations aren't serving us well?

Let's try a thought experiment.

Think back to any time before you were 20 years old:

What did you love to do?

What activities — games, hobbies, sports, extracurricular events, or school subjects — did you enjoy? Recall your natural, uncoerced proclivities.

Think about what kept you absorbed for hours and made you happily oblivious to the rest of the world. What tasks made time fly?

Write down your thoughts on the following page.

Core Interests
to the Fore!

Do you still indulge in those happy activities or something similar? Are they still part of your Wheel of Life?

Just as Buckingham observes, many of us gave up "childish" activities to pursue the serious business of studying, working, or otherwise preparing to make our livelihoods as responsible adults.

Perhaps believing that childhood passions were at odds with satisfaction as adults, we abandoned them for conventional goals.

But, while people certainly do change and adapt over time, research suggests that our core personality traits, passions, and interests remain relatively stable from childhood onward.[7]

So even when we have achieved conventional "success," we — like Carol, the tax attorney in the story on page 126 — often harbor unrealized dreams rooted in the activities we chose as children.

If, as adults, we fail to recognize and pursue core interests in some form, we may live out our lives without experiencing full satisfaction and fulfillment.

"Each of us carries within a secret yearning—
a yearning that, as time and life march on,
often becomes a secret sorrow. That yearning
will be different for each of us, as it is the most
deeply longed-for expression of self. Only to
the degree that we — each of us — are able to
bring forth our own heart's core will our lives
feel fulfilled, truly worthwhile."
— George Kinder [8]

Multiple Roles

You've reflected on your work, your interests, and your childhood. Now use the following exercises to think about defining yourself in a way that helps move your work life forward.

Dick Bolles, arguably the world's most influential career counselor, created a powerful way to help answer the crucial "Who am I?" question.

Take ten blank sheets of paper. At the top of each, write "Who Am I?"

Then, on each sheet, write one answer to that question.

When you have finished, go back over all ten sheets and expand what you've written. Write (1) *why* you said that, and (2) *what excites you* about that answer.

When you're finished, review and arrange the sheets in priority order. In other words, which identity is most important to you? Put that page on top. Which identity is next? That goes beneath the top sheet. Continue until the least important identity is at the bottom of the stack.

Finally, go back over the ten sheets, in order, and look carefully at how you described *what excites you*. See if there are any common denominators among your ten responses. If so, jot them down on a separate piece of paper.

Voilà! You're starting to put your finger on some things that your dream job, career, or mission needs to give you if you are to feel excited, fulfilled, and useful.[9]

The next page shows how one Forum member completed this exercise.

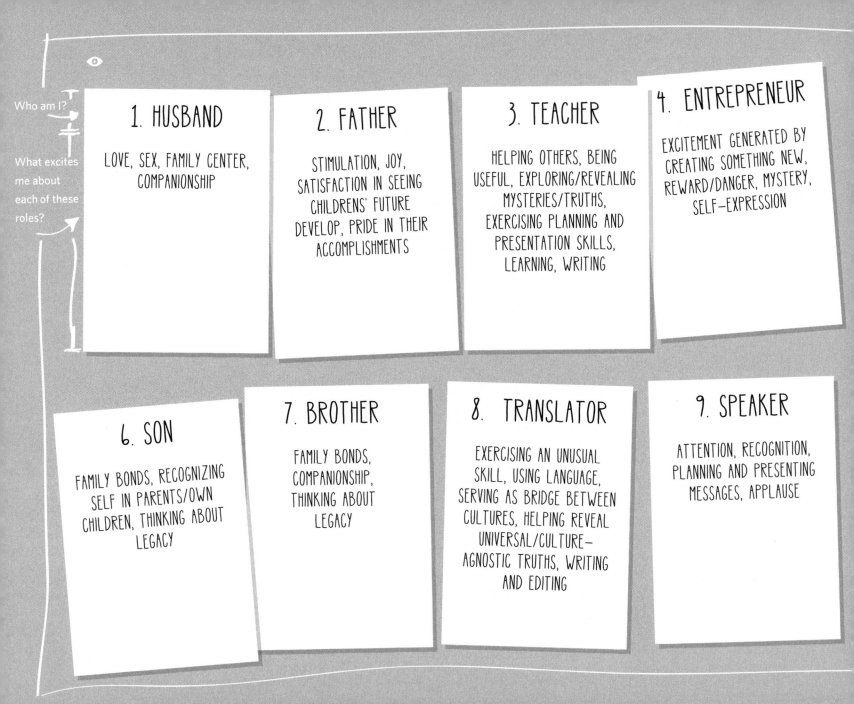

Who am I?

What excites me about each of these roles?

1. HUSBAND

LOVE, SEX, FAMILY CENTER, COMPANIONSHIP

2. FATHER

STIMULATION, JOY, SATISFACTION IN SEEING CHILDRENS' FUTURE DEVELOP, PRIDE IN THEIR ACCOMPLISHMENTS

3. TEACHER

HELPING OTHERS, BEING USEFUL, EXPLORING/REVEALING MYSTERIES/TRUTHS, EXERCISING PLANNING AND PRESENTATION SKILLS, LEARNING, WRITING

4. ENTREPRENEUR

EXCITEMENT GENERATED BY CREATING SOMETHING NEW, REWARD/DANGER, MYSTERY, SELF-EXPRESSION

6. SON

FAMILY BONDS, RECOGNIZING SELF IN PARENTS/OWN CHILDREN, THINKING ABOUT LEGACY

7. BROTHER

FAMILY BONDS, COMPANIONSHIP, THINKING ABOUT LEGACY

8. TRANSLATOR

EXERCISING AN UNUSUAL SKILL, USING LANGUAGE, SERVING AS BRIDGE BETWEEN CULTURES, HELPING REVEAL UNIVERSAL/CULTURE-AGNOSTIC TRUTHS, WRITING AND EDITING

9. SPEAKER

ATTENTION, RECOGNITION, PLANNING AND PRESENTING MESSAGES, APPLAUSE

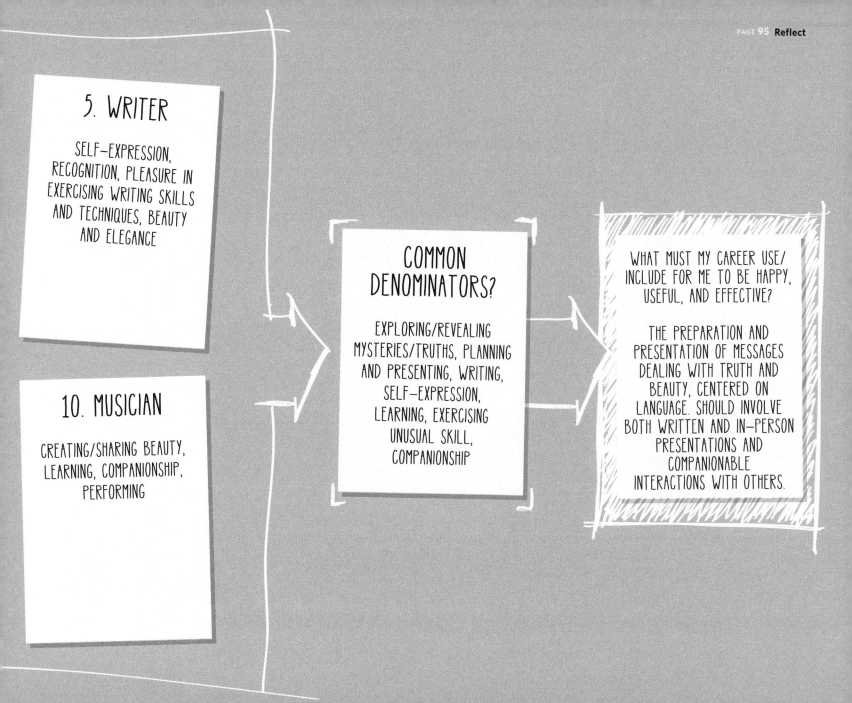

5. WRITER

SELF-EXPRESSION, RECOGNITION, PLEASURE IN EXERCISING WRITING SKILLS AND TECHNIQUES, BEAUTY AND ELEGANCE

10. MUSICIAN

CREATING/SHARING BEAUTY, LEARNING, COMPANIONSHIP, PERFORMING

COMMON DENOMINATORS?

EXPLORING/REVEALING MYSTERIES/TRUTHS, PLANNING AND PRESENTING, WRITING, SELF-EXPRESSION, LEARNING, EXERCISING UNUSUAL SKILL, COMPANIONSHIP

WHAT MUST MY CAREER USE/ INCLUDE FOR ME TO BE HAPPY, USEFUL, AND EFFECTIVE?

THE PREPARATION AND PRESENTATION OF MESSAGES DEALING WITH TRUTH AND BEAUTY, CENTERED ON LANGUAGE. SHOULD INVOLVE BOTH WRITTEN AND IN-PERSON PRESENTATIONS AND COMPANIONABLE INTERACTIONS WITH OTHERS.

Multiple Canvases

Once you've defined and prioritized your different roles, consider this notion: You could draw a separate Canvas for each.

For example, if you drew a Canvas illustrating your role as a spouse, who would your Customer(s) be? What Value would you Provide? Through which Key Activities?

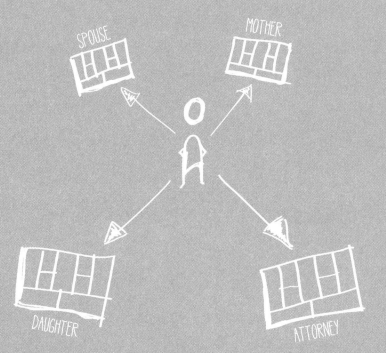

Kristiina: A Truly Personal Business Model

☐ Old Model   ☐ New Model

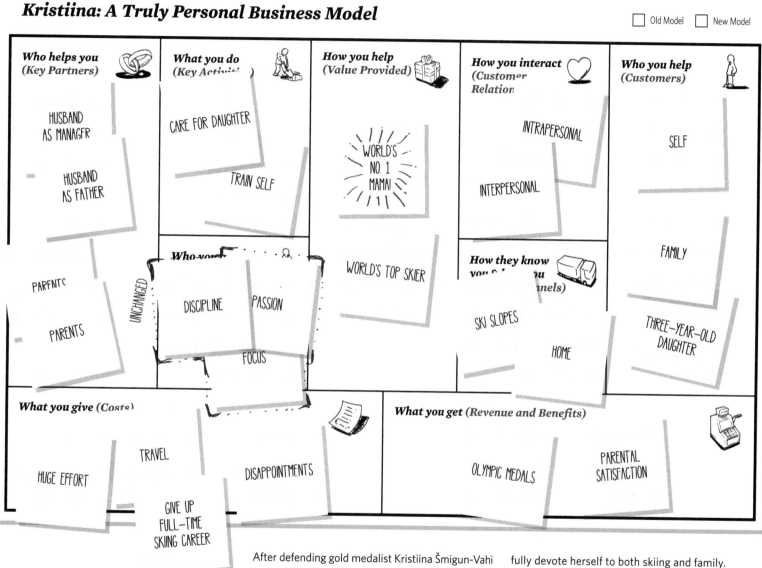

Who helps you (Key Partners)

HUSBAND AS MANAGER

HUSBAND AS FATHER

PARENTS

PARENTS

What you do (Key Activities)

CARE FOR DAUGHTER

TRAIN SELF

Who you are

UNCHANGED

DISCIPLINE   PASSION

FOCUS

How you help (Value Provided)

WORLD'S NO. 1 MAMA!

WORLD'S TOP SKIER

How you interact (Customer Relations)

INTRAPERSONAL

INTERPERSONAL

How they know you & how you (Channels)

SKI SLOPES

HOME

Who you help (Customers)

SELF

FAMILY

THREE-YEAR-OLD DAUGHTER

What you give (Costs)

HUGE EFFORT

TRAVEL

DISAPPOINTMENTS

GIVE UP FULL-TIME SKIING CAREER

What you get (Revenue and Benefits)

OLYMPIC MEDALS

PARENTAL SATISFACTION

After defending gold medalist Kristiina Šmigun-Vahi took the silver in freestyle cross-country at the 2010 Winter Olympics, she decided it was impossible to fully devote herself to both skiing and family. She redrew her personal business model with a new Purpose: becoming the world's No. 1 Mama!

Lifeline Discovery

Most career professionals agree that work satisfaction is driven by three key factors: interests, skills and abilities, and personality.[10]

The Lifeline Discovery is a tool that helps you define and examine these factors.

a. Plot Your High and Low Points

Recall events representing high and low points in your life, and plot them on a timeline that stretches back as far as you can remember.

The vertical axis represents enjoyment and/or excitement; the horizontal axis represents time.

"High points" and "low points" are:

- Specific, important events in your life: good or bad, personal or professional — whether related to work, social life, love, hobbies, academics, spiritual pursuits, or other areas
- Milestones or landmarks you remember clearly and are associated with strong feelings
- Key career changes, both positive and negative

Below is a blank "Lifeline" you can use (or draw your own). For now, plot each event on your Lifeline with a point and a short description, such as "married Jan" or "got job at Vesta."

Start at the far left with the earliest high or low point you can remember, and then work toward the present. When you've plotted 15 to 20 events, draw a line connecting all points.

Your Lifeline may now look something like the one at right by Darcy Robles, a Forum member who completed the exercise to help clarify how satisfied she was with her work situation.

Excitement/Enjoyment

My Lifeline

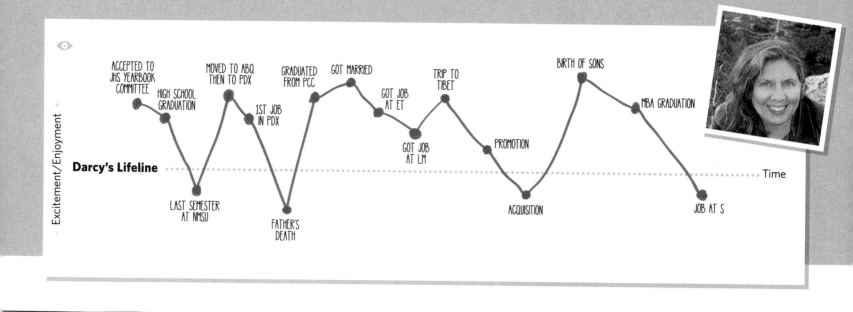

Darcy's Lifeline

Excitement/Enjoyment

ACCEPTED TO
JHS YEARBOOK
COMMITTEE

HIGH SCHOOL
GRADUATION

MOVED TO ABQ
THEN TO PDX

1ST JOB
IN PDX

GRADUATED
FROM PCC

GOT MARRIED

GOT JOB
AT ET

TRIP TO
TIBET

BIRTH OF SONS

MBA GRADUATION

GOT JOB
AT LM

PROMOTION

Time

LAST SEMESTER
AT NMSU

FATHER'S
DEATH

ACQUISITION

JOB AT S

Time

b. Describe the Events

Write a concise sentence or two describing each event. The idea is to capture some of the key work satisfaction drivers mentioned earlier, specifically interests, abilities/skills, and values. Some guidelines:

Use action words, such as "designed," "led," or "assembled." Try to describe each event using two or more verbs. For example, if you delivered a solo rendition of a song at a school assembly, rather than "sang song," write *selected, rehearsed, and performed 'Don't Let the Rain Come Down' at schoolwide talent show. Drew big applause!"*

As part of this step, include a note about the *context* in which you acted—in other words, write down the place and theme of the event. In the example above, the context is "schoolwide talent show."

Here's how Darcy Robles described five of her events:

1. Accepted to yearbook committee: Worked as a part of a group to design and develop junior high school yearbook. Learned importance of positive thinking, having confidence in myself.

2. Graduated from Portland Community College with computer information systems degree: Found great satisfaction using logical/reasoning skills to solve problems, learned to design/develop solutions, enjoyed contributing ideas/working with groups toward common goal.

3. Job at IT as primary IT person: Listened to problems/opportunities from internal customers, got deep satisfaction from using technical/analytic skills to develop solutions. Continually increased technical knowledge thanks to working in variety of areas, enjoyed the high energy, optimistic atmosphere.

4. Trip to Tibet: Enjoyed the adventure, uniqueness of Tibetan culture. Enjoyed increasing my knowledge of the people and their history. Period of self-reflection and personal growth.

5. Employer changes due to acquisition: Managed a team of people/day-to-day operations, little technical development. New ideas/ability to implement them constrained. Some personal development, but not much new learning. New company culture more bureaucratic, old-style management, more money —than value-driven, less positive energy.

My Lifeline Events:

1

2

3

4

5

6

7

8

9

10

11

12

13

14

15

16

17

18

19

20

c. Recognize Interests

Now it's time for some fun self-discovery.

Interests are a Key Resource that truly make you
you. Consider all your high point events — the
things that excited you. In what context (industry
sector/theme/interest area) did each event occur?
What activities or actions were involved? What
other commonalities point to specific interest
areas? Incidentally, how do the interest areas suggested match up with your Wheel of Life results?

Another idea to consider: Identify career transi-
tions *where you made the key decisions regarding
the change*. Were these mostly career highs or
career lows?

Career professionals note that an *internal locus
of control* is crucial to career satisfaction. Internal
locus of control means *you* decide for *yourself*
what you want to do, rather than being influenced
by external parties (family, friends, colleagues,
money, society at large). When we know ourselves
well, we're unlikely to act in response to others'
expectations — or leave our careers on autopilot.

What Darcy Recognized

I've been most satisfied when I was able to use my creative and analytical (logical and reasoning) skills to develop and implement solutions to those problems in a positive, solution-oriented atmosphere. I have gotten deep satisfaction from contributing to a project with a hard-working team with a common goal or working with customers to develop solutions to their problems. Finally, a common theme is variety and continual learning, both on skills and personal growth/development.

My key verbs: Develop, create, solve, learn, analyze, implement ideas, communicate, work with others

d. Identify Skills/Abilities

Return to your Lifeline Event list on page 103 and circle the high points. Then, review the table below. Check cells with words that describe activities you did in your high points. Few of the words will *precisely* describe your activities, so check ones that are *similar*. Then, tally each column's checks.

CHECKS START HERE!

Accounting work		Advertised		Analyzed		Assembled		Attended/ organized event		Debated	
Audited		Artistic creativity		Conducted independent research		Built structure		Belonged to social club		Initiated action	
Data processing		Conceptualized		Developed questions		Cared for animals		Cared for children, senior citizens		Led people	
Figured/ calculated		Created artwork or publication		Diagnosed		Drove vehicle		Coordinated		Negotiated	
Inventoried		Created ideas		Entered science fair or contest		Electrical/ mechanical repair		Counseled		Participated in political campaign	
Managed office		Designed building or furniture		Investigated		Repaired object		Empathized		Persuaded/influenced	
Operated machinery		Dramatized		Laboratory work		Scheduled		Hosted		Promoted	
Programmed computer		Edited		Read technical or scientific publications		Surveyed or navigated		Interviewed		Ran own business	
Purchased		Performed music or dance		Solved technical or scientific problem		Took vocational course		Made friends		Sold	
Recorded/ transcribed		Took arts-related course		Study specialized subject		Troubleshoot equipment		Participated in religious service		Spoke in public	
Secretarial work		Took photographs		Took science course		Used tools/heavy equipment		Taught, instructed		Supervised/ managed others	
Took business course		Wrote/published		Wrote or edited technical article		Worked outdoors		Volunteered		Took management course	

TALLY UP EACH COLUMN

e. Top Ten and Favorite Five

Rank your top ten activities by counting the total number of check marks in each cell.

Top Ten Activities

1

2

3

4

5

6

7

8

9

10

Next, identify your five favorite activities, regardless of how many check marks they received. Take a look at what you wrote down for part b on page 102. Are any of those activities your favorites? Did they all receive many check marks, or are some of them items that you'd like to spend more time with?

My Favorite Five Activities

1

2

3

4

5

f. Define What You *Can* and *Want* to Do

From your Top Ten and Favorite Five lists, identify three to five activities that you're excited about — and capable of — using at work.

Can and Want to Do

1

2

3

4

5

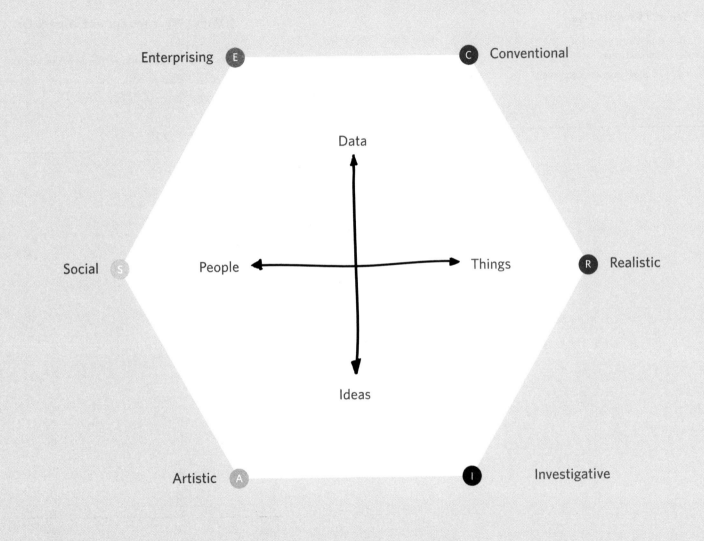

Personality and Environment

This exercise, based on a well-known career assessment and counseling methodology, helps you understand work choices in terms of your personality — as well as environments that harmonize (or conflict) with it.[11]

John Holland was a U.S. psychologist whose theories about career choices have been tested and validated by many researchers over several decades. Holland's theories form the basis for the world's most widely used vocational interest inventory and for various United States Department of Labor classifications and publications.

Decades ago, Holland had a key insight that today seems obvious: Vocational interests are an expression of personality. In other words, *occupations represent a way of life — an environment rather than a set of isolated work functions or skills.*[12]

This means that people express their personalities through career choices, just as they express their personalities when selecting friends, hobbies, recreation, and schools. Equally important, it means that career satisfaction depends on a good match between a worker's personality and the work environment (important note: "work environment" means primarily *other people at the workplace*).

To help people understand vocational interests as an expression of personality, Holland defined six different personality tendencies (types), emphasizing that every person is a *mix* of multiple tendencies. Some tendencies are simply more prominent than others.[13]

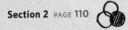

Holland's Six Tendencies

Social

Prefers working with people to inform, develop, help, or cure. Interpersonal/educational ability. Tends to avoid activities demanded by realistic occupations or situations.

Investigative

Prefers investigating/researching physical, biological, or cultural phenomena. Scientific/mathematical ability. Tends to avoid activities demanded by enterprising occupations or situations.

Artistic

Prefers manipulating physical or intangible materials to create art forms or products. Artistic/language/musical ability. Tends to avoid structured activities or conventional occupations.

Speech Notes to the Team

C Conventional
Prefers organizing/processing data in structured situations. Clerical/computational ability. Tends to avoid ambiguous, free, unstructured occupations or situations.

E Enterprising
Prefers influencing/leading others to achieve organizational goals or economic gain. Leadership/persuasion ability. Tends to avoid investigative occupations or situations.

R Realistic
Prefers working with tools, machines, or animals, often outdoors. Mechanical/athletic ability. Tends to avoid activities demanded by social occupations or situations.

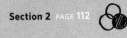

Uncover Your Key Personality Tendency

To sharpen your understanding of your own personality tendencies, look back at the table on page 106. The six personality tendencies are color-coded in the Activity columns: red, blue, yellow, aqua, green, and purple. Each color represents one of the six personality tendencies.

Write your column totals from page 106 next to the corresponding colors in the hexagon on page 113. If you checked more blue words than any other, your leading personality tendency is "Investigative."

Understanding the six tendencies not only helps us better understand ourselves — it helps us better understand our working environments, which are composed primarily of *other people*.

In fact, work environments, like people, can be described using the six tendencies. A bank is a good example of a Conventional environment, while an advertising agency is a good example of an Artistic environment. Career satisfaction depends in large part on compatibility between the work environment and the worker's personality.

For instance, people with strong Artistic tendencies are likely to become dissatisfied in Conventional work environments such as banks or insurance companies. Similarly, a Conventional worker is unlikely to thrive in an Artistic workplace such as an advertising agency or theater. Who you are (Key Resources) "drives" what you do (Key Activities); the two must harmonize.

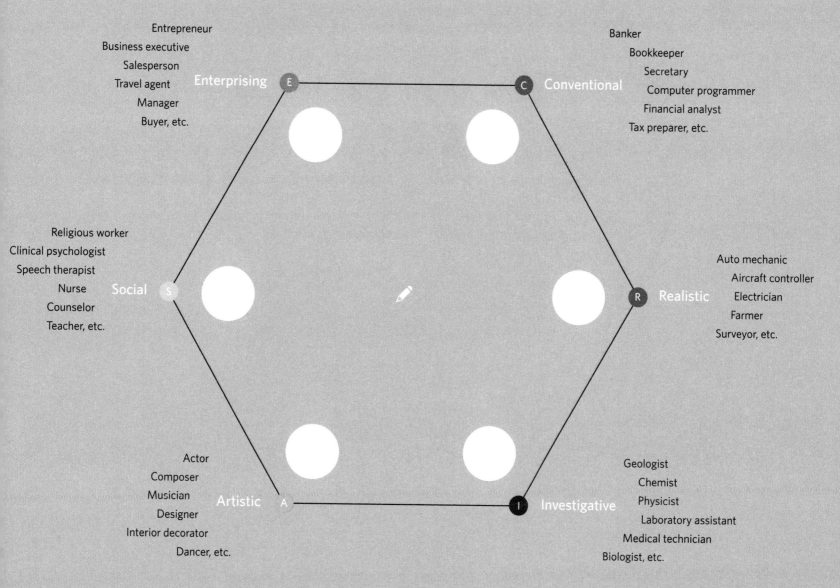

Enterprising — E

Entrepreneur
Business executive
Salesperson
Travel agent
Manager
Buyer, etc.

Conventional — C

Banker
Bookkeeper
Secretary
Computer programmer
Financial analyst
Tax preparer, etc.

Social — S

Religious worker
Clinical psychologist
Speech therapist
Nurse
Counselor
Teacher, etc.

Realistic — R

Auto mechanic
Aircraft controller
Electrician
Farmer
Surveyor, etc.

Artistic — A

Actor
Composer
Musician
Designer
Interior decorator
Dancer, etc.

Investigative — I

Geologist
Chemist
Physicist
Laboratory assistant
Medical technician
Biologist, etc.

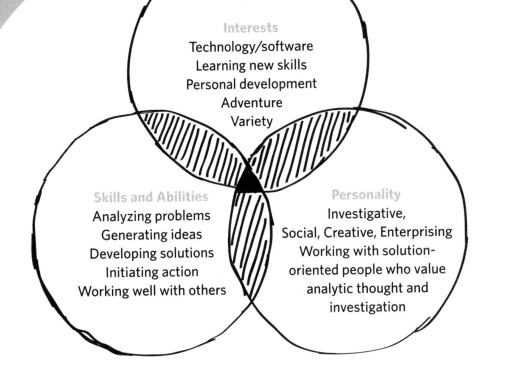

Interests
Technology/software
Learning new skills
Personal development
Adventure
Variety

Skills and Abilities
Analyzing problems
Generating ideas
Developing solutions
Initiating action
Working well with others

Personality
Investigative,
Social, Creative, Enterprising
Working with solution-
oriented people who value
analytic thought and
investigation

"I realized that I enjoy analyzing and problem-solving, but it's important that I have the ability to work with and help others and to create, develop, and implement ideas and solutions."
—Darcy Robles

KNOW YOURSELF

THE COMPUTER PROGRAMMER

Sometimes adjusting the "fit" between worker and workplace environment can dramatically boost satisfaction, as Sean Backus might tell you.

In college, Sean took a full-time courseload while working 15 to 20 hours per week as a computer programmer. He excelled at programming, both as a computer science major and at his part-time job. Sean's professors praised his expertise and encouraged him to explore and advance. What's more, his employer, software developer Credence Systems, liked his work so much that the company offered him a full-time job upon graduation.

Sean took the job with Credence. He knew and liked programming and was thrilled with the opportunity to launch a career immediately after graduating.

But Sean was surprised to discover that working at Credence wore him down. Attributing it to having joined the wrong company, he quit and took a programming job at a different software firm. But he soon grew frustrated there, too, and moved on to a third employer. Now, he was experiencing similar feelings yet again.

At this point, Sean was angry — and desperate. Within two years of graduating, he had quit two jobs and started a third. He questioned whether he had selected the right course of university study. At a loss, he sought help from a professional career counselor. She recommended spending several weeks focusing not on a new job search, but on learning more about Sean Backus, the person. He agreed.

Using interviews and assessment tools, the counselor helped Sean identify his strong Social tendencies. In fact, Sean discovered he was at heart a "people person" who happened to have strong natural mechanical abilities. During college, interactions with peers and faculty had met his social needs, while the part-time programming job had been a keen personal interest and a welcome source of income. But as a full-time employee, sitting in front of a computer screen all day drained and frustrated him.

Sean realized that, while he enjoyed technology, he lacked sufficient social interaction at work and needed to deal more with people. After discussing the situation with his employer, he was able to transition to a position that involved teaching computer skills to other employees. His work satisfaction soared.

Sean learned how Key Resources interplayed with other elements of his personal business model:

Interests, skills, and abilities

Sean's computer-related interests, skills, and abilities were genuine — and an important Key Resource. So until he became overly frustrated with full-time programming work, Sean had felt little need for self-discovery. Once he did reflect, though, he discovered other important interests, skills, and abilities, particularly *facilitating* and *instructing*. These Key Activities were completely missing from his work life, something that was pushing up "soft" Costs in the form of frustration and dissatisfaction.

Personality

Sean learned about the Conventional "programmer" side of his personality, but also discovered that his Social tendencies slightly outweighed his Conventional inclinations. Programming-only jobs frustrated him because the immediate work environment harmonized with only one aspect of his personality: the Conventional tendency toward structure, organization, and predictability.

Locus of control

Sean enjoyed computers but never deliberately defined himself as a programmer. Rather, peers, professors, and colleagues forged the definition of "Sean the programmer" through their praise and affirmation. This encouragement, plus Credence's unsolicited full-time job offer, made it natural for Sean to adopt the "programmer" definition as his own without reflecting on its truth. This adoption was so complete that Sean attributed his career problems to external sources (employers) rather than to internal sources (mismatch between Key Resources and Key Activities resulting from lack of self-knowledge).

LEARN FROM ANOTHER'S PERSPECTIVE

THE PREMED STUDENT

The decision to pursue medicine was Khushboo Chabria's alone. She hadn't been prodded by family or friends; in fact, her parents had hoped that following graduation from a less-challenging undergraduate program, she'd quickly settle into a new life as a wife and mother.

Still, Khushboo's heart had been set on becoming a doctor for years. And determined as she was, she enrolled as a premed at the University of California at San Diego.

As it turned out, Khushboo's independence and resolve overshadowed a serious mismatch between her goals and her true nature.

Insight struck during an interview for a lab position with an organic chemistry professor. The professor asked Khushboo about her extracurricular experience, including a six-month Washington, D.C., internship involving health care reform.

"Your eyes shine when you talk about your internship, but not when you talk about science," the professor noted. "It doesn't seem like you're in the right place."

Khushboo started realizing that the things she'd cared about and enjoyed — the health care internship, working on an emergency student housing program, her part-time marketing job at the campus activities office — were fundamentally different from the activities involved in becoming, and practicing as, a physician.

The real epiphany came during a late-night coffeeshop conversation with a friend. "You're not doing what you really want to do," he insisted. "You're not a person who belongs in a white coat."

Khushboo stalked away furious — then realized she was angry because her friend had been right. Her Social and Enterprising tendencies far outweighed her Investigative inclinations.

"Growing up I didn't recognize that the things you need to learn to become a doctor were not sufficiently interesting to me," she says. "I wouldn't have been able to discover who I am without help from others pointing out which activities really satisfy me."

Khushboo is now a human development major/psychology minor whose post-graduation aspirations involve a mix of social psychology, innovation, and public policy.

Spend time with a "trusted other"

Khushboo's experience shows how powerfully a trusted third party can help with career-related decisions. We've designed *Business Model You* to serve to some extent as your trusted other. But when it comes to self-discovery, nothing can replace deep, face-to-face dialogue with family, friends, colleagues, or career guidance professionals.

What Sort of Person Are You?

Here's a simple but powerful self-discovery exercise you can do with a friend, colleague, supervisor, parent, or other partner who has insight into your personality and character.

1. Make a few copies of the personal qualities list on pages 122–123. On one copy, circle the personal qualities that best describe you. Keep going until you have a dozen or so.

2. Describe what the selected words mean to you. If you circled *Steady*, for example, you might write "I always stick with a project to the very end and rarely get sidetracked."

3. Give a fresh, unmarked copy of the word list to a trusted friend, colleague, employer, family member, or other partner. Ask this person to circle a dozen or more words he or she believes describe you well. Here's one way to introduce the exercise:

"I'm trying to get a sense of how other people see me. Can you circle a dozen or so words that describe me well from your perspective?"

4. Talk with your partner about why they circled particular words. You might start the discussion like this:

"You circled *Creative*. How does my creativity show itself? How important would you say creativity is to me as a person? What else should I know about why you circled *Creative*?"

5. Repeat the exercise with as many trusted others as is practical. After three or four sessions, some common themes should emerge. How do others' perceptions of you align with your self-perception? You may discover personal strengths you never recognized![14]

Abstract thinker	Boring	Curious	Emotional
Academic	Broad minded	Customer-focused	Empathetic
Accepting	Business like	Daring	Energetic
Accurate	Calm	Decisive	Enterprising
Achievement driven	Carefree	Defeated	Enthusiastic
Action-orientated	Careful	Deferential	Exceptional
Adaptable	Caring	Defiant	Exciting
Adventurous	Cautious	Deliberate	Expedient
Affectionate	Changeable	Dependable	Experienced
Afraid	Charismatic	Dependent	Expert
Aggressive	Cheated	Depressed	Firm
Aggrieved	Cold	Detail-orientated	Flexible
Aloof	Commercially aware	Determined	Focused
Ambitious	Committed	Diligent	Foolish
Amused	Competent	Diplomatic	Forgiving
Analytical	Competitive	Disappointed	Forthright
Angry	Confident	Disciplined	Friendly
Annoyed	Confused	Discreet	Frustrated
Anxious	Conservative	Disdainful	Fun-loving
Appreciative	Consistent	Dismayed	Generous
Apprehensive	Content	Disorganised	Gentle
Articulate	Cool	Dominant	Gloomy
Ashamed	Cooperative	Down to earth	Grateful
Assertive	Courageous	Dynamic	Grounded
Astute	Crazy	Easygoing	Guarded
Authoritative	Creative	Efficient	Happy
Bashful	Credible	Effective	Helpful

Helpless	Literate	Persuasive	Resourceful	Stimulating	Trapped
Hostile	Lively	Pioneering	Responsible	Straightforward	Triumphant
Humiliated	Logical	Pleased	Responsive	Strategic thinker	Trusting
Humorous	Lost	Positive	Risk taking	Strong	Unassuming
Hysterical	Loving	Practical	Sad	Successful	Understanding
Idealistic	Loyal	Pragmatic	Satisfied	Sulky	Unique
Imaginative	Matter-of-fact	Precise	Sceptical	Supportive	Unsettled
Impatient	Mature	Predictable	Scornful	Surprised	Unusual
Impulsive	Methodical	Private	Self-assured	Suspicious	Vengeful
Indecisive	Mild	Proactive	Self-controlled	Sympathetic	Versatile
Independent	Mischievous	Protective	Self-critical	Tactful	Vicious
Indifferent	Modest	Proud	Self-motivated	Talented	Vigorous
Individualistic	Motivated	Punctual	Self-reliant	Talkative	Visionary
Industrious	Objective	Questioning	Self-righteous	Task-orientated	Warm
Influential	Open	Quick	Sensitive	Team builder	Wary
Initiative-taker	Orderly	Quiet	Serene	Team player	Weak
Innovative	Organised	Rational	Serious	Tenacious	Willful
Insightful	Outgoing	Reactive	Shy	Tender	Witty
Intellectual	Outstanding	Realistic	Silly	Tense	Worrier
Introspective	Overly-sensitive	Reflective	Sincere	Theoretical	
Jealous	Panicky	Rejected	Slow	Thick-skinned	
Joyful	Patient	Reliable	Sociable	Thin-skinned	
Judgemental	Peeved	Relieved	Sophisticated	Thorough	
Kind	Penetrating	Remorseful	Sorrowful	Tidy	
Knowledgeable	Perceptive	Resentful	Sorry	Timid	
Lacking ambition	Persevering	Reserved	Spontaneous	Tolerant	
Light-headed	Persistent	Resilient	Steady	Traditional	

Defining Work, Defining Ourselves

What's work to you?

We may not be on the cusp of a layoff. We might not even feel burnt out. But for whatever reason, many of us are on career autopilot — as Andrea was before losing her job. We're cruising along more or less smoothly, but our direction and speed is set more by momentum than intention. We may even be satisfied to the extent that our work is built upon core interests. But satisfaction often fades when we fail to pilot our own planes.

One way to discover whether you're on autopilot — and help further develop the self-reflection process — is to think about work's current place in your life and whether that place matches work's true meaning to you.

Despite our assorted dimensions (which we just explored!), many of us define ourselves primarily by our jobs. Strangers often break the ice by asking, "So, what do you do?"

As it turns out, work can have very different meanings for different people. And what works means to you is a big part of *who you are*.

Traditionally, experts have ascribed three meanings to work:

Work as Job

This means working for the sake of a paycheck, without much personal involvement or satisfaction.

Roy Baumeister describes this way of thinking in *Meanings of Life*: "The job is an instrumental activity — that is, something done principally for the sake of something else."

Still, jobs can produce valuable feelings of skill and satisfaction, not to mention sustenance that enables a worker to pursue meaning in other areas of life.

Work as Career

Work as career is motivated by the desire for success, achievement, and status. The careerist's approach to work is not a passionate attachment to the work itself, Baumeister writes. Rather, it "emphasizes the feedback about the self that comes in response to work. For the careerist, work is a means of creating, defining, expressing, proving, and glorifying the self." Work as career can be an important source of meaning and fulfillment in life.

Jane Smith
~~Vice~~ President

For example, people with "jobs" may derive more meaning and satisfaction from family, hobbies, religion, or other non-work activities.

"Careerists," on the other hand, tend to have much of their life's meaning invested in work. Some may sacrifice family or other interests in order to rise in the world and achieve more prestige, wealth, or recognition.

Work as Fulfillment

Work as fulfillment is best described as a strongly interest-driven (or even passionate) approach to work — but one lacking the overwhelming, all-encompassing nature of a "calling." People pursuing work as fulfillment may choose unconventional career paths that favor personal interests over financial reward, recognition, or prestige. Such work can be an important source of meaning in life.

Some who are "called" may experience great spiritual fulfillment and vocational success. Yet others may suffer deprivations unknown to the conventionally employed (fine artists and missionaries come to mind).

Work as Calling

As mentioned in the story about Carol on the next page, the word "calling" derives from the idea that one is "called upon" to do a certain type of work: either externally, by God or community, or internally, by a natural gift demanding expression. It's done "out of a sense of personal obligation, duty, or destiny," Baumeister says.

In addition to these traditional three categories, we suggest a fourth: Work as Fulfillment.

Clearly, these four categories overlap, and any one person's work may contain elements of each. The categories, though, suggest how work can furnish us with more or less meaning in our lives.

Finally, those working for fulfillment may find much of life's meaning in work, perhaps without sacrificing family and other interests.

A Message
to the Unsure

Robert Symons, a psychotherapist and London-based career counselor, smiled empathetically as Carol, a tax attorney, broke down sobbing.

Mr. Symons had just asked his client the trigger question: What had become of the spontaneous, excited child she must once have been?

Later, when asked about the scene, Mr. Symons noted he'd seen it replayed countless times over the years.

What lay behind Carol's emotional response — and similar responses by many others? Mr. Symons explained that:

. . . the most common and unhelpful illusion plaguing those who came to see him was the idea that they ought somehow, in the normal course of events, to have intuited — long before they had finished their degrees, started families, bought houses and risen to the top of law firms — what they should properly be doing with their lives.[15]

Mr. Symons went on to describe how his clients were "tormented by a residual notion of having through some error or stupidity on their part missed out on their true 'calling.'"

In other words, people believed they were meant to pursue a particular career path — one where they'd both excel and feel satisfied — but had failed to find it.

Where do people get this idea?

The notion of "calling" originated in medieval times, and referred to a sudden encounter with a heaven-sent command to devote oneself to Christian teachings. According to Symons, a non-religious version of this idea survived, and continues to trouble much of today's workforce. Symons's interviewer describes the notion as:

. . . prone to torture us with an expectation that the meaning of our lives might at some point be revealed to us in a ready-made and decisive form, which would in turn render us permanently immune to feelings of confusion, envy and regret.[16]

Many people feel that, even if they lack a true "calling," they're somehow not optimizing their work lives. How can they address such concerns? As a professional career counselor, Mr. Symons points to a reassuring idea from the humanist psychologist Abraham Maslow:

It isn't normal to know what we want. It is a rare and difficult psychological achievement.
— Abraham Maslow

How do you spend most of your time?

For many of us, it's a huge relief to learn that not knowing what we want is normal rather than exceptional.

Many people find it comforting to recognize that:

- There is no single or correct "meaning" of work
- Life offers many sources of satisfaction and fulfillment, both related and unrelated to work
- Our ideas about work — and our abilities to do certain work — change with age
- You are not defined by your work — unless you want to be

We all decide for ourselves the extent to which we identify with our career; there are no right or wrong answers. But many find persuasive writer Leil Lowndes's suggestion that we replace the clichéd conversation-starter "What do you do?" with a far more inviting question that honors anyone's self-definition: How do you spend most of your time?[17]

- What role does work play in your life today?

- Is it a job, career, calling, or fulfillment? A combination?

- How does work's current place in your life match your beliefs about its true meaning?

CHECKING IN: WHERE WE'VE BEEN SO FAR

Up to this point, we've discussed business model thinking, the basics of financial sustainability, and why all organizations — for-profit, nonprofit, and social — must abide by the logic of earning a livelihood.

We saw how business model thinking helps organizations — and individuals — reinvent themselves in response to changing social, economic, and technological trends.

Then, we covered how you can use the Canvas to describe your personal business model.

In this chapter, you re-examined your important (multiple!) extra-work roles, the core interests, skills and activities you find satisfying, your key personality tendencies, how work environments have their own "personalities," the importance of engaging trusted others in the self-discovery process, and work's meaning and place in your life.

WHERE WE GO FROM HERE

It's time to address the most fundamental question underpinning business models, whether organizational or personal.

It's a simple question that's extraordinarily challenging to answer: What is your purpose?

CHAPTER 5
Identify Your Career Purpose

PURPOSE TRUMPS SKILLS

THE HISTORIAN

Adrian Haines believes in the power of the past. He holds a Master of Science in medieval history and has worked in or with museums for most of his professional life. Five years ago, he moved to the suburbs of Amsterdam for a dream job: helping a publisher of historical books conceive and create new titles under partnerships with museum curators and librarians. But as time passed, two things made Adrian realize he needed to reinvent his career.

First, he'd grown frustrated with his employer's reluctance to embrace digital publications and social media. Second, his wife missed living in the city and was eager to move back.

Adrian learned that a large national library was accepting applications for a "digitization project leader." Adrian sensed the position was an excellent match for his background and interests, but believed he lacked the management skills needed to work for a larger, more bureaucratic organization. So he consulted Forum member Mark Nieuwenhuizen for help reconceiving his personal business model.

Mark's first observation was that Adrian was too focused on details, specifically whether he had the professional and managerial skills needed to execute the job. So Mark suggested Adrian focus on his Purpose and Value Provided.

After some consideration, Adrian recognized that his Value Provided — and his true passion — was "rescuing history from dusty museum and library walls and putting it in places where everyone can enjoy it." The insight helped him understand his frustration with his current employer and articulate his conviction that history can be appreciated not only through print and physical facilities, but through digital media, as well.

As Adrian prepared to apply for the new position, Mark urged him to focus less on his *skills* and more on how his Purpose matched what the library *needed*. Working with the Canvas, Adrian recognized that his newly articulated Purpose opened up several potential growth paths. For example, many of Adrian's current and past Customers were museums, so he had a network through which he could seek work as the general manager of a mid-sized museum or as a curator in a larger museum.

Adrian was scheduled to interview for the new position just as *Business Model You* went to press. Whatever path he takes, he now recognizes that Purpose trumps skills:

"It's amazing how many professional possibilities appear when you use Value and Purpose — rather than skills — as starting points for reinventing your career."

SEA OF JAPAN

KOREA

Kanazawa

Tokyo
Yokohama

H O N S H U

Fusan

FUJIYAMA

Nagoya
Biwa
Kyoto

Korea Strait

Kobe
Osaka

Hiroshima

Tsushima Strait

34° N

OCEAN

Nagasaki

KYUSHU

PASSPORT

United States
of America

4. 旅先で予定しているアクティビティーは、出発前にどの程度計画しますか？

○ あまり事前には計画しない
● ほとんどのアクティビティーを事前に計画する
○ ある程度のアクティビティーは事前に計画する
○ ほとんど事前に計画することはない

5. 出発前にアクティビティーを計画する場合、オンラインメディアをどの程度活用していますか？

○ あまりオンラインメディアを活用しない
○ ほとんどの情報をオンラインメディアで入手する
○ ほとんどオンラインメディアは活用しない

6. 海外旅行の際、ショッピングに関して出発前にどんな情報を準備していますか？（複数回答可）

□ ショッピングをする場所の確認
□ ショップリストの用意
□ 買い物リストの用意

WHEN IT'S NOT ABOUT YOU

THE ENTREPRENEUR

The company I started did research and market entry consulting for companies wanting to enter Asian markets, particularly Japan. After more than six years of ferociously hard work, we received a multi-million-dollar buyout offer. This was all new to me; when I started, I didn't even know people sold companies.

Anyway, I paid off three mortgages, maxed out the kids' college funds, took the family on a great vacation, and invested the remainder to provide passive income. But like everyone else, I still faced the big question: What am I going to do with the rest of my life?

In a way, that question grew tougher precisely *because* I'd been relieved of the pressing need to earn a living. Seeking answers sharpened my awareness that work is about more than achieving financial independence.

I think most successful entrepreneurs feel the same way. I've talked with a lot of people who collectively have sold dozens of companies for amounts ranging from one to $40 million U.S. Not a single one ever mentioned "achieving financial independence" as their primary motivation for working.

Fortune-seekers can rarely sustain their passion through the hard times. Successful enterprises are laser-focused on Value Provided to Customers. Entrepreneurship is not about you; it's about effectively serving others.

Raise Your Purpose Flag!

Let's revisit the simile we introduced in Chapter 2: Business models are like blueprints. They guide construction of a business, much as a blueprint guides construction of a building. Now, let's extend the comparison.

In order to create a blueprint, the architect must understand the Purpose of the building to be constructed.

For example, if the tenants will be doctors and dentists, the building needs to be designed to accommodate waiting areas, examination rooms, a lot of sinks and bathrooms, and heavy, wall-mounted equipment, such as x-ray machines.

Purpose is equally important when creating an organization or business from scratch. The organization's Purpose guides the design of its business model. In that sense, Purpose is a crucial "off-Canvas" element. It is also a significant design constraint: After all, no organization — or building — can be designed to be all things to all people.

The same holds true for personal business models. Modifying or reinventing a personal business model calls first for clarifying its underlying Purpose. Consider Purpose a "meta layer" guiding your personal business model from above. Raise your Purpose flag high!

"If you don't realign your work with your purpose, you're just going to relocate that problem to another desk." — Bruce Hazen

Conversely, aligning work and Purpose jump-starts careers — and makes satisfaction soar.

Where to begin

On the previous page, Carl James notes that entrepreneurship is about serving others. We, too, suggest that the overarching Purpose of our lives is helping others. As successful entrepreneurs know, even someone whose Purpose is to amass a fortune can only succeed *by selling services or products that help people in some way*.

But how do you recognize and/or shape your overarching Purpose? The next three experiments can help you answer that crucial question.

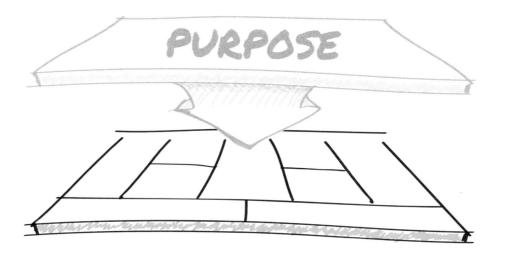

Cover Story You!

This exercise was created by David Sibbet.[18] It challenges the imagination and helps participants link purpose and core interests.

Imagine that it's two years from today, and a major media outlet has just run a big story about you, featuring quotes and a photo of your smiling face. Wow!

1. What is the name of the media outlet? Choose an actual magazine, newspaper, or program you would be proud to be featured in.
2. What is the story about? Why are you featured?
3. Write down some quotes from the interview. You could even create a collage with quotes, insets (sidebars), pictures cut out from magazines, or diagrams.

This exercise is especially effective for groups of three or more who can share and discuss their "cover stories."

THE TEACHER

NAME

MEGAN LACEY

EXERCISE:

COVER STORY YOU!

1. I'm being interviewed by Terry Gross on National Public Radio's *Fresh Air* to talk about an after-school running program I started at my local high school. The program began as an effort to improve attendance rates and motivation levels.

2. In the beginning, I simply met with a handful of students at the track — every day after school — and helped them train for a race. As time went by, more students joined, and I added more components to the program. Students volunteered at races; community members helped with transportation and training. Eventually, I worked with the school to integrate ideas from the running program into the school's core curriculum.

   Attendance rates and motivation levels increased. Unexpectedly, so did scores on state tests — as well as the school's graduation rate. As a result, several other districts picked up the program.

3. NPR: You started out with just a few students — how did you manage to recruit even a couple?

   I promised to pay the race entrance fee for anybody who came to every session. When you say you'll pay for something, kids listen.

"The students needed to see that school has immediate application — it's more than preparation for those seemingly far-off goals of college and jobs."

"They stayed out of trouble, they stayed healthy, and they connected with the community and the curriculum."

npr FIND A STATION | SEARCH [___] GO
home | news | arts&life | MUSIC | programs | listen | news | podcasts

Recommended (26,727)

Running Away With Education Reform

Audio for this story from *Fresh Air* will be available at approx 5:00 pm ET — Transcript

Oct 24, 2016 — text size A A

As it turns out, the first step toward education reform may not begin inside a classroom at all.

Megan Lacey, a high school teacher in Washington state, seems to think it starts with a pair of shoes and the

CLARINDA ECCLES · TJ TALALEY
Food cart Dilemma
NOW PLAYING IN SELECT THEATERS

most popular

1. Running Away With Education Reform
2. The Least Boring Auditor in the World
3. Are You Afraid of ...

141

The Three Questions

Here's another exercise ideal for undertaking with a partner or small group. Participants can jot down their thoughts, then share with others and discuss.

1. Think back to several times when you felt fulfilled (revisit the Lifeline Discovery exercise on page 99 to recall specific events). What were you doing? Why did it feel so good? Describe those feelings as specifically as you can.

2. Name one or more of your role models. Who do you admire most, and why? Write down several words that describe that person. For example, one Forum member named Nelson Mandela as a role model. While doing this exercise, she wrote down *kindness, persistence in the face of adversity, recognition,* and *status.* These words offered clues to the things she valued in herself as well as others.

3. How would you like to be remembered by your friends? Write down some of the things you hope they'll say about you after you're gone.

THE TECHNICAL TRAINER

EXERCISE:

THE THREE QUESTIONS

QUESTION 1:

I felt fulfilled while working at a software company, particularly while training colleagues and partners. I was able to teach what I knew and, at the same time, learn from other people's experiences. I think we all perceived the impact on each other's lives.

QUESTION 2:

My role model is Zilda Arns, a Brazilian pediatric doctor who died in the 2010 Haiti earthquake. She was recognized for her kindness, solidarity, and dedication to combat infant mortality, malnutrition, and domestic violence.

QUESTION 3:

I'd like to be remembered as good-humored, dedicated, passionate, and honest—someone who loved his family, who allowed himself and others to express their emotions, and who had the courage to reinvent his personal life and work by finding new meaning.

Your Brand-New Life

One day, you're surprised by a courier who hands you a thick packet of legal documents. Rich, eccentric Uncle Ralph has died and left you $18 million, but you must fulfill two conditions to receive the money.

Uncle Ralph's will calls for you to quit your job and pursue two one-year tasks. During these two years, you'll receive a monthly living allowance plus reimbursements for expenses related to accomplishing the tasks, such as travel and education. At the end of the first year, you'll receive a lump sum of $9 million and another $9 million in a trust fund to be released upon completion of the second yearlong task.

1. First Year, First Task

Spend this year learning new things. You're NOT required to attend a college, university, or any other formal educational program. You simply must use your time and energy to focus intently on learning new things. So, what would you learn? How would you develop yourself?

2. Second Year, Second Task

Find a cause to support. You have one year to investigate, participate in, and ultimately select a cause or a project you really care about — something that will help humanity (your neighborhood/city/country/the world/ the environment, etc.). At the end of the second year, you must donate the $9 million in your trust fund to the cause or project you've selected. What cause will you select?

— Epilogue —

Your Lifestyle Starting in Year Three

What sort of lifestyle will you enjoy after completing the two tasks? You have $9 million. Where will you live? With whom? How will you spend your time? What activities will you pursue? What will you strive to accomplish?

THE SEEKER

EXERCISE:
BRAND-NEW LIFE

New Things I Would Learn

I embrace Swami Rama's approach to enlightenment, as described in his book *Living With the Himalayan Masters:* "Let the world be little to you. Let you be on the path of spirituality." Here are specific inquiries I'll explore:

- Study Portuguese and take an extended trip to Brazil.
- Learn how to finish and sell one of dozens of book ideas I've had over the years.
- Learn the skills required to become a master multimedia storyteller: videography, Web and blog design/content strategies, and music recording.
- Improve my personal fitness: cycle three days per week, do Yoga and dance, and adjust my diet to support these activities.

My Chosen Cause

I regularly ask myself, "How can I strip down my material existence that I might get back to real living?" In my search for answers, I came across Jiddu Krishnamurti, an Indian-born philosopher and educator trained in the intellectual traditions of both East and West. I believe Krishnamurti's message about human relationships and social change should be heard on a broader scale, so I'll help spread Krishnamurti's ideas by working with and supporting the Krishnamurti Foundation.

The Rest of My Life

Three years from now, I'll be living in a small home purchased in the Santa Teresa district of Rio de Janeiro. My Portuguese will be strong enough to build relationships with emerging Brazilian enterprises looking to market their products in the U.S. I'll use my mastery of the language along with now-expert digital storytelling skills to generate business partnerships with these companies, and I'll volunteer my time to help impoverished Brazilians acquire the resources and skills to support themselves and improve their living conditions.

You've created some terrific raw material to help
identify your career Purpose. Now it's time to craft a:

Purpose Statement

Imagine you are financially independent — as you did in the previous
exercise — and ready to start living *exactly* as you choose. Jot down
your thoughts about this new life right on the pages of this book,
using the three squares that follow:

Activities

Describe three or four activities you will most enjoy focusing on.

People

Describe several people or groups of people with whom you'd like to spend your time.

Helping

How will you help other people? Use three or four action words (verbs) to describe specifically how you'll help others.

Use the following not-very-grammatical sentence as the foundation for your Purpose Statement:

"I would like to HELP PEOPLE through these ACTIVITIES."

Next, fill in the following table with the verbs and nouns you wrote in the squares on pages 146-147. Put your favorite verbs and nouns first!

I'd like to	help (verb)	people (noun)	by doing activity (verb)

There you have it! You've created some powerful (though maybe nonsensical) sentences that point toward an authentic, satisfying Purpose. Consider this your first draft of a Purpose Statement. You'll want to play around with the sentences and rearrange the words, but you get the idea.

Here's how one *Business Model You* Forum member started crafting her Purpose Statement:

I'd like to	help (verb)	people (noun)	by doing activity (verb)
	inspire	restless professionals	making
	support	recent grads	organizing
	empathize	young creatives	nurturing
	remember	my heroes	sharing

To make her Purpose Statement logical from a vocational standpoint, she left her partner (her first priority) out of the table's 'people' column. While her sentences didn't make perfect sense, their underlying message was clear and powerful, and she revised to create the following Purpose Statement:

I'd like to help restless professionals and young creatives improve their lives by inspiring and supporting them.

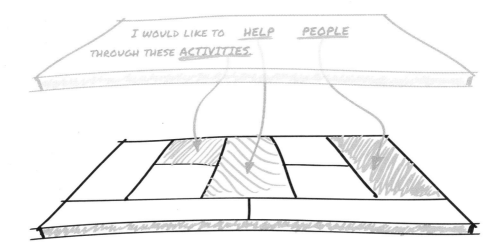

I WOULD LIKE TO _HELP_ _PEOPLE_ THROUGH THESE _ACTIVITIES_.

Putting Purpose into Play

You may have noticed how the Purpose Statement
resembles the personal Business Model Canvas:

Help means *Value Provided*

People means *Customers* (and coworkers)

Activities means *Key Activities*

Your Purpose Statement is a crucial step toward redefining
your personal business model based on the *Activities* you would
like to carry out to *Provide Value* to *Customers*.

"Those who are not prepared for the apprehension of a great purpose should fix the thoughts upon the faultless performance of their duty, no matter how insignificant their task may appear. Only in this way can the thoughts be gathered and focused, and resolution and energy be developed, which being done, there is nothing which may not be accomplished."

— James Allen, *As a Man Thinketh*

What If You Can't Define Your Purpose?

What if you have trouble defining your Purpose? First, recognize that you're hardly alone:

Only **three percent** of all people have the courage to find and follow their dreams, according to one writer.[19]

Second, you can still achieve excellence and satisfaction by concentrating deeply on whatever work you do.

The Ever-Changing Purpose Statement

Co-creators of this book who worked through these exercises more than once often found the results changed within the space of several months.

It's helpful to recognize that Purpose changes over time — and for different reasons. Life stage is one reason: Age 20 concerns (establishing a career, finding a significant other, etc.) are completely different from age 55 concerns (seeing children make the transition to adulthood, leaving a legacy, etc.). Big life events (marriage, divorce, births, deaths, new jobs, illness, etc.) are another reason for changes in Purpose. Finally, while our core interests and abilities tend to remain stable over time, *the form of their expression* may evolve.

As co-creator Laurence Kuek Swee Seng put it, "the Purpose Statement is a perpetual work in progress." He recommends keeping a working Purpose Statement on file — and updating it regularly as your life and perspectives change.

Goals vs. Purpose

Many of us have goals in life: short-, medium-, or long-term. But how many of us enjoy true *Purpose*?

Goals differ from Purpose. Entrepreneur Oki Matsumoto makes the distinction by advising organizations to "aim for the North Star, not the North Pole."[20]

Matsumoto's point is that the North Star represents an organization's *vision*: a guiding force that continuously aligns everyone's efforts. In contrast, the North Pole represents a goal that must be achieved or reached — and once that occurs, replaced again and again with a new destination.

Stephen Shapiro applies similar thinking to individuals in his provocatively titled book *Goal-Free Living*. Shapiro encourages readers to "use a compass, not a map," and to "meander with purpose." The idea is to maintain a sense of direction rather than strive for a specific destination — to gather new information as you move forward, and, based on that information, either confirm that your direction is true or course-correct.

BMY Co-creators Raise Their Purpose Flags!

我希望可以帮助各专业人士、企业家以及学生追求合资企业与各项目.通过明确、优化及强化他们实现目标的努力.成为他们的顾问、教练或合作者.

郭瑞承

Laurence Kuek Swee Seng
Malaysia

Me gustaría ayudar a profesionales cualificados con problemas de empleabilidad, con pocos conocimientos empresariales y habilidades de gestión, a __repensar__ su futura vida profesional y __reiniciar__ su carrera.

FERNANDO SÁENZ-MARRERO

Fernando Sáenz-Marrero
Spain

To open dialogue to expand a person's capacity to love and be lovable.

Kat Smith
United States

I will help the {UNDERVALUED + UNDERPRIVELEGED} become EMPOWERED to improve {THEIR OWN + OTHERS'} lives through mentoring, collaborating and birthing innovative impact-ful solutions.
-E

Emmanuel A. Simon
United States, via Trinidad and Tobago

I'D LIKE TO SUSTAIN COMPANIES AND ORGANIZATIONS THROUGH THE INNOVATION OF BUSINESS PROCESSES.

—MICHAEL ESTABROOK

Michael Estabrook
United States

My purpose is to evolve the female entrepreneur so that she may turn her intellectual capital into multi-generational wealth.

Kadena Tate

Kadena Tate
United States

Ik help ondernemers, investeerders businesscoaches en consultants bij het ontwikkelen van succesvolle bedrijven door complementaire ambities, netwerk en ervaring te verbinden èn te faciliteren

Marieke Post, "Ambition Angel"

Marieke Post
Netherlands

Me levanto todos los días, para revolucionar el mundo a través del diseño de experiencias extraordinarias e innovadoras que cambien para bien la vida de las personas. Para lograr esto es vital enseñar a la gente que la felicidad precede al éxito. Al final es acerca de hacer felices a otros.

Alfredo Osorio Asenjo
Chile

THE ACID TEST

Can you confidently and proactively share your Purpose Statement with others? If you lack confidence or feel embarrassed, you've got more work to do.

When you've got it right (at least for the time being), then it's time to move on to the Revise stage — and explore possibilities for reinventing your personal business model using your newly crafted Purpose Statement as a guide.

Revise

Adjust — or reinvent — your work life using the Canvas and discoveries from previous sections.

CHAPTER 6
Get Ready to Reinvent Yourself

Mountain View, California
A roomful of giggling Google employees is standing, hands overhead, swaying from side to side. Their speaker has asked them to do this if they recognize any of their own internal monologues in a series of PowerPoint slides:

"You contemplate your life and where you are going and the question 'Is this all there is to it?' arises unbidden and makes you uncomfortable."

☐ Yes ☐ No

"You constantly plan to set your life straight 'when' something happens or something gets over — *when* that big project you are working on is completed, *when* your mother recovers from surgery and leaves the hospital, *when* your child gets straight, *when* your job-hunting spouse finds one."

☐ Yes ☐ No

"You evaluate all events in terms of their impact on you. If your spouse gets a great job offer you wonder how it will impact your relationship or if your boss gets fired you wonder if you will get that job or how you will get along with whoever comes next."

☐ Yes ☐ No

Srikumar Rao, a jovial presenter with an infectious laugh, goes on to explain how we all live amidst a constant stream of internal chatter — chatter that reinforces our "mental models" of how the world works. With a knowing nod to the wave of shrugs, squints, and head-scratching that follows, Rao continues: "All of you are living in a dream world."

A murmur ripples through the crowd.

"Your entire life, including the reality you are experiencing," he says, "is a set of stories that you have told yourself and continue to tell yourself."

At these words, a few attendees, apparently discovering urgent messages on their Blackberries, exit the room. But most stay. And forty minutes later, more than a few leave with their perspectives on life fundamentally altered.[21]

Altering Your Perspective

Rao, who believes that "it is important to learn how to strive mightily while remaining serene," claims that none of his ideas are original. Everything he presents, he says, derives from millennia-old spiritual and philosophical traditions dealing with fundamentals of the human condition.

Maybe that's why his message resonated so poignantly among workers at Google, the epitome of intellectual and technological might. Even in a lightspeed digital era, it seems, how we live and work is ultimately shaped by timeless human elements.

And it's the human elements we must address when preparing to modify our personal business models. Everyone longs for freedom from self-defeating mental chatter, and who hasn't dreamed of self-reinvention?

Let's begin with a variation of a beautiful thought experiment invented by the great British philosopher Bertrand Russell in the early 1900s.

Imagine 20 people simultaneously viewing a chair (a). Every single one of the 20 viewers sees the chair differently.

Some people see the chair like this (b). Others have this view (c). A tall person might see (d).

In other words, there could be 20 different perspectives of the same chair.

Are all of these perspectives accurate? Yes.

Well, then if they are all accurate, which one *is* the chair? Hmmm.

The answer? None of them. All perspectives are merely *representations* of the chair, not the chair itself. And while the chair itself may be a single reality, people experience it in strikingly different ways.

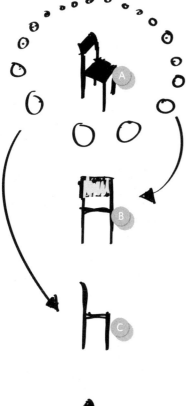

In fact, our *perception* of the chair affects us more than the actual reality of the chair itself. Therefore, meaningful experience of the chair is based on a mere representation (our perspective) — not the actual chair.

Russell's point was this: We can never fully see or completely know the chair's physical reality in its totality, even though we know such a reality exists. Our viewing perspective always limits our knowledge.

However!

If you walked around the circle of viewers and stood momentarily behind each person to gaze at the chair, you yourself would see different perspectives of the chair.

So if 20 people can have 20 perspectives on the chair, you can change your own view of the chair — simply by shifting your perspective.

In short, you wield the power to reconceive reality.

As a Man Thinketh

Here's the kicker: Reconceiving reality can change reality.

Everything you perceive about your career, your love life, and your family and friends, is not necessarily reality, it's merely your *perception* of reality. And your perception represents only one possible reality — one of 20 views of the chair — not the *only* reality.

Problems arise when we assume that the "reality" we perceive (reinforced by mental chatter such as *I'm failing in my career, my boss hates me, jealous colleagues are undermining my efforts*, etc.) is *the* reality.

In a significant way, the world as we experience it is not real. Rather, says Rao:

"We invented it. We constructed it out of bits and pieces. We made it out of our mental models and then lived by their dictates. And having done all this, we proceeded to carry on with our lives without ever realizing that our mental models were made up merely of perceptions, not facts."[22]

Transcending Mental Models

When preparing to reinvent a personal business model, it can be helpful to practice freeing ourselves from self-imposed constraints. You may be familiar with the following exercise, which often helps participants begin thinking about mental models —unspoken assumptions—that are failing to serve them effectively.

Create the nine-dot pattern to the right on a separate sheet of paper, or simply do the exercise right here on this page:

1. Join all nine dots
2. Draw no more than four straight lines
3. Do not lift your pencil from the paper
4. Lines may be drawn at any angle
5. When you're done, every dot must have a line passing through it

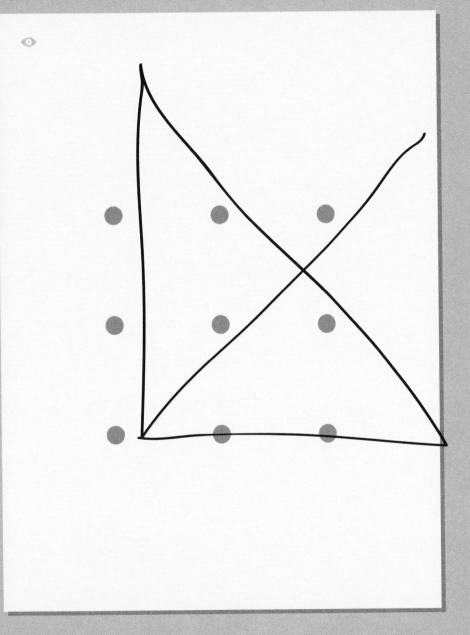

The solution (quite literally) is to *think outside the box.*

The unspoken assumption most of us make — our "mental model" regarding this puzzle — is that we must *stay within the frame bounded by the nine dots.* But the puzzle is impossible to solve within the confines of that assumption. As Benjamin and Rosamund Zanders wrote, the confines are all invented:

"**The frames our minds create define — and confine — what we perceive to be possible. Every problem, every dilemma, every dead end we find ourselves facing in life, only appears unsolvable inside a particular frame or point of view. Enlarge the box, or create another frame around the data, and problems vanish, while new opportunities appear.**"[23]

Here's another reality-bending puzzle.

Make the equation at right true by
adding a single unbroken line:

An easy solution is to draw a vertical line through
the "equals" sign to create ≠. But there's another
solution — can you find it?

$$5 + 5 + 5 = 550$$

$$5 + 5 + 5 = 550$$

It's easy to dismiss the notion that reality is "invented" as feel-good, New Age nonsense. What's important, though, is that the "it's all invented" perspective is profoundly *useful* — regardless of whether it's objectively *true.*[24]

Rao suggests another exercise to help you work on mental models (your perception of reality) that are failing to serve you well.

The Editor

Grab a paper and pencil, and set aside at least ten minutes of quiet time for yourself.

Now, think of a situation that's bothering you and describe it on paper.

Read how Forum Member Amber Lewis described her own situation, then try imagining a new reality as she did.

"Our staff writers don't respect me. They keep turning in stories with the same problems, even though I send e-mail after e-mail explaining how to avoid those problems — and why it's crucial to do so. They're ignoring my instructions. Maybe I'm too young for this position, or maybe I'm not cut out for leadership at all."

Reinforced by compatible mental chatter, Amber constructed this "reality" around her situation — recurring problems with writers' work — and believed it more and more strongly as time went by.

When this happens, it's time to come up with an *alternative* reality: one that explains the same situation but serves you far more effectively.

Here's the alternative reality Amber imagined:

"Some of the writers are new to the company and might still be adjusting to our style and the tough workload. Plus, I've only interacted with them by e-mail — it can be easy to misinterpret or miss the point when communication is entirely online."

Rao emphasizes that your alternative reality should:

1. **Be better than the one you are experiencing now.**
2. **Be one that you can plausibly accept.**

Once you've selected a plausible, preferable alternative, abandon your earlier perception and adopt the new reality. Live as if it were true.

As you live this alternative reality, says Rao, immediately acknowledge and dwell upon every scrap of evidence that it is working. Resolutely ignore contradictory evidence. You may feel as if you are playacting. You are correct. You are! Eventually you will become the role you are trying to play.

To help adopt her new reality, Amber decided to arrange in-person meetings with the writers so that she could review company style, answer questions, and provide clarification and guidance on issues that were unclear or difficult to address through e-mail. The result? The true situation turned out to be far closer to Amber's alternative, preferred reality.

INVENTING SOMETHING BETTER

Think of the personal Business Model Canvas as a modeling tool for reconceiving reality in ways that better serve you. Keep in mind that redefining a personal business model can be chaotic. For one, compared with organizations, people have *more* non-work priorities and *fewer* clear goals. Yet organizations — despite *fewer* non-work priorities and *more* clear goals, struggle with business model innovation:

The challenge [. . .] is that business model innovation remains messy and unpredictable, despite attempts to implement a process. It requires the ability to deal with ambiguity and uncertainty until a good solution emerges [. . .]. Participants must be willing to invest significant time and energy exploring many possibilities without jumping too quickly to adopt one solution.[25]

CHAPTER 7
Re-Draw Your Personal Business Model

TURN "WEAKNESSES" INTO STRENGTHS

THE GREEN ADVOCATE

Not everyone loves his politics, but former Vice President of the United States Al Gore is an extraordinary example of re-examining Purpose, perspective, and identity — and, as a result, successfully reinventing a personal business model.

Gore's renewal began after the 2000 presidential election. He won the popular vote by a margin of more than half a million, but lost the election when a legal controversy over vote recounting in Florida led the Supreme Court to rule in favor of George W. Bush. Disillusioned with public office, Gore lamented that "What politics has become is something that requires [. . .] tolerance for artifice and manipulative communications strategies."[26] He resolved to "democratize television" by founding Current TV, a company whose user-generated content business model was revolutionary for cable television in 2002. Redoubling his longtime passion for environmental issues, he then launched an investment fund focused on corporations committed to economic and environmental sustainability.

Gore's reinvention peaked with the 2006 release of *An Inconvenient Truth*, an Academy Award-winning documentary featuring his PowerPoint presentation about global warming. As a politician, Gore had struggled for nearly three decades to publicize threats to Earth's ozone layer. But it took a new personal business model to achieve his goal: the film attracted worldwide attention and transformed Gore into a media superstar and a leading advocate for environmental causes.

Several factors made Gore's personal business model reinvention successful:
- Renewed focus on core interests: Gore's passion for environmental causes — a weakness as a politician — became his greatest strength as a private citizen
- Helping more Customers: Gore extended his Customer base far beyond the United States — and to new, non-political sectors
- Adopting new Channels: Film, DVDs, and books converted Gore's Value Provided from a service into products that could reach far more people

Al Gore's Personal Business Model Transformation

☐ New Model

Key Partners

POLITICIANS
HEADS OF STATE
STAFF, ADVISORS, ETC.

SCIENTISTS

INVESTORS   BUSINESSPEOPLE

PRODUCERS

MEDIA OUTLETS

Key Activities

CONFER WITH PRESIDENT,
KEY PARTNERS
READ LEGISLATIVE DRAFTS, MEMOS,
REPORTS, ETC.
WRITE MEMOS, CRITIQUES,
CORRESPOND, SPEAK, ETC.

PRESENT   WRITE BOOKS,   INVEST
ARTICLES

Re:

PASSION FOR PUBLIC SERVICE
JOURNALIST BACKGROUND
ENTERPRISING/SOCIAL PERSONALITY
TENDENCIES

INVEST IN PROMISING
"GREEN" FIRMS

Value Provided

SERVE AND PROTECT
U.S. PUBLIC
ASSUME PRESIDENCY IN
EMERGENCY

LEAD CLIMATE
CHANGE AWARENESS
INITIATIVES

SERVE, PROTECT
ENTIRE WORLD

PROVIDE CITIZEN
MEDIA PLATFORM

Customer Relationships

IN-PERSON, PHONE, E-MAIL,
WRITTEN REPORTS, ETC.
RETENTION FOCUS

TRADITIONAL AND
ONLINE MEDIA   ACQUISITION FOCUS

Channels

SPEECHES, PRESS CONFERENCES
REPORTS, BOOKS

MOVIE, DVDS,   LECTURES
ONLINE MEDIA

Customers

UNITED STATES CITIZENS
PRESIDENT BILL CLINTON

CITIZENS,
GOVERNMENTS
WORLDWIDE

ENTREPRENEURS

CORPORATIONS

Costs

TIME, ENERGY, STRESS, LACK OF PRIVACY
POLITICALLY–IMPOSED CONSTRAINTS ON
SPEECH, ACTION

CRITICISM FOR
"SELLING OUT"

Revenue and Benefits

SALARY, BENEFITS
RECOGNITION, SATISFACTION IN
PROVIDING PUBLIC SERVICE

MOVIE ROYALTIES   STOCK OPTIONS

SPEAKING FEES   EARNINGS
DISTRIBUTION   SATISFACTION OF
TACKLING TRULY
GLOBAL ISSUES

ELIMINATE
POLITICALLY–IMPOSED
CONSTRAINTS
ON ACTION

Redraw Your Personal Business Model

What follows are five steps to help you pair insights from Chapters 4 through 6 with a set of crucial reinvention tools — and guide you toward a brand new Canvas.

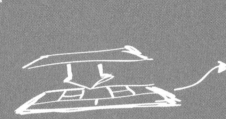
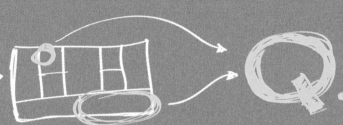

1. Draw Your Personal Business Model as It Stands Today

Remember your Chapter 3 version? Draw it again here or on a separate sheet of paper. This time, guided by your Purpose, you should be able to more powerfully articulate Who You Are, How You Help, and Who You Help.

2. Identify Pain Points

Where does your work life hurt? Using the Canvas you just drew, circle the building blocks where you feel dissatisfied.

For example, if you want to make more money, circle the Revenue building block. Or if you dislike selling — yet that's one of your most important activities — circle the Key Activities building block *as well as* the specific element "selling."

3. Ask Diagnosis Questions

Next, answer the questions about your most painful building block(s) on the following pages. Some of the questions address problems; others point to potential opportunities. Either way, look under "Solution Starting Points" for hints about the kinds of actions you might want to take.

The Personal Business Model Canvas

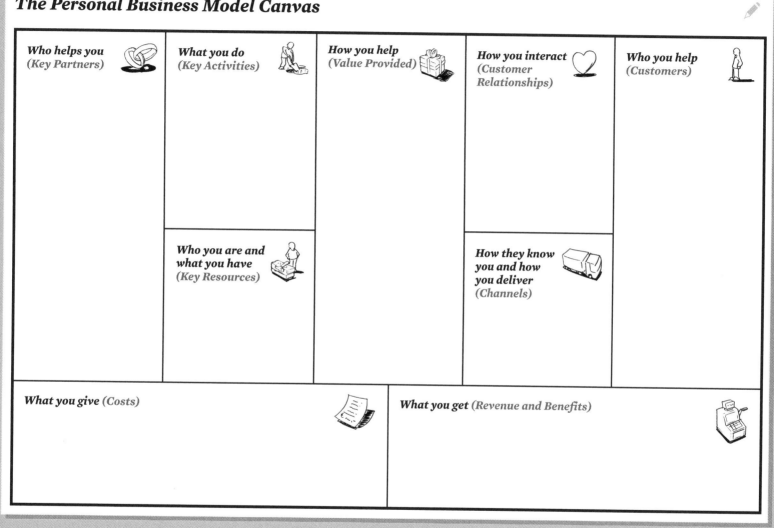

Who helps you
(Key Partners)

What you do
(Key Activities)

How you help
(Value Provided)

How you interact
(Customer Relationships)

Who you help
(Customers)

Who you are and what you have
(Key Resources)

How they know you and how you deliver
(Channels)

What you give *(Costs)*

What you get *(Revenue and Benefits)*

Diagnosis Qs

Who You Are and What You Have
What You Do

Questions	Solution Starting Points
Are you interested in your work?	If so, great! If not, there's probably a fundamental mismatch between **Key Resources** (Who You Are) and **Key Activities** (What You Do). You also may want to reconsider your Purpose. Revisit Chapters 4 and 5.
Are you underutilizing or *not* using an important ability or skill?	A missing or underused ability or skill incurs **Costs** in the form of stress or dissatisfaction. Can you add that ability or skill to your **Key Activities** to support or improve your **Value Provided**? Revisit Chapters 4 and 5 to examine *why* you are underutilizing that skill.
Do your personality tendencies match your workplace? (Remember, "workplace" is largely defined by the people you work with). Do your personality tendencies match your work activities?	If so, terrific! If not, consider acquiring new **Customers** (or **Key Partners**) with more compatible personality tendencies. Customers are linked to **Value Provided**, so check **Value Provided** diagnosis questions on the next page. Check Chapter 4 to make sure your personality harmonizes with your work activities.

Who You Help

Questions	Solution Starting Points
Do you enjoy your **Customers**?	If so, great! If not, imagine the qualities a "dream" **Customer** would have. Can you find such clients in the sector you're now working in? If not, consider revising your model.
Who is your most important **Customer**?	Define why this **Customer** is so important. Is it hard Benefits? Soft Benefits? A combination of both? Does this **Customer** justify a new or distinct **Value Provided**?
What is the true job the **Customer** is trying to get done? Does the **Customer** have a "bigger picture" reason or motivation for engaging your services? For example, is your immediate **Customer** serving another, larger **Customer** who has a bigger job-to-be-done?	Can you reconceive, reposition, or modify your **Value Provided** to help the **Customer** succeed with a bigger job?
Is serving the **Customer** too expensive? Is serving the **Customer** driving you crazy?	Are **Costs**, including soft **Costs**, too high to justify serving this **Customer**? Is **Revenue** (or **Benefits**) too low? Can you afford to fire the Customer? Can you afford *not* to fire the **Customer**? Work through **Value Provided**, **Costs**, and **Revenue** and **Benefits** diagnosis questions.
Is the **Customer** equating **Key Activities** with the job-to-be-done? Are you?	Sometimes **Customers** themselves haven't clearly defined jobs-to-be-done. Can you help them define it? Can you redefine or modify **Key Activities** to boost **Value Provided**?
Do you need new **Customers**?	If so, consider changing your **Customer Relationships** focus from retention to acquisition. Do you need to do more selling or marketing? Improve or develop your skills in this area? Find **Key Partners** who can help you acquire new **Customers**?

How You Help

Questions	Solution Starting Points ✎
What elements of your services are truly valued by the **Customer**?	Ask the **Customer** this question — the answer may surprise you. Work through **Customer** diagnosis questions on page 181.
Does your **Value Provided** address the biggest, most important elements of the **Customer's** job-to-be-done?	Do you understand the true job-to-be-done, or are you guessing at what it is? Can you reconceive/reposition or modify your **Key Activities** to focus more sharply on crucial **Value Provided** elements?
Could you deliver your **Value Provided** through a different **Channel**?	Does your **Customer** prefer the current **Channel**? Could you adapt **Value Provided** for alternative delivery **Channels**? Could you change your **Value Provided** from a service into a product, thereby creating a scalable business model (see page 45)?
Do you enjoy delivering your **Value Provided** to **Customers**?	If so, great! If not, revisit **Key Resources** and consider overhauling your model.

How They Know You and How You Deliver 🚚 *How You Interact* ♡

Channels Questions

Solution Starting Points

How do **Customers** find out about you?

How do **Customers** evaluate your services (or product)?

Do you enable **Customers** to buy in the way(s) they prefer?

How do you deliver your service/product?

How do you ensure post-purchase satisfaction?

Have you clearly *defined* how you help so you can *communicate* how you help? In what new ways could you create awareness or encourage evaluation (social media, online presentations, etc.)? Are you enabling purchase and delivery in ways **Customers** prefer?

Can you offer different purchase options? Can you deliver through a new or different medium (DVD, podcast, video, in-person)? Could a **Key Partner** build awareness or deliver on your behalf? Have you asked **Customers** how satisfied they are with your service or product?

Through which **Channel**(s) do you now create awareness and deliver **Value Provided**? Do you deliver directly to **Customers**?

Is it possible to convert your service into a product, thereby making possible delivery to many more **Customers**? (This is the key to creating a scalable business model; see **Value Provided** diagnosis questions).

Customer Relationships Questions

Solution Starting Points

What kind of relationships does the **Customer** expect you to establish and maintain?

Are you communicating with **Customers** in ways they prefer — or in ways you prefer? Consider adding, removing, growing, or reducing one (or more) communication method.

Which is the primary goal of your **Customer Relationships**: retention or acquisition?

If your primary goal is retention, does one of your **Key Activities** gauge **Customer** satisfaction? (If satisfaction is low, see **Value Provided** diagnosis questions.) If your goal is acquisition, do you need to add or grow selling or marketing-related **Key Activities**?

Would establishing or joining a user community improve communication with your **Customer**? Could you co-create a service or product with your **Customer**?

Could your **Customers** help each other — or could you automate **Customer Relationships** to some extent — through a user community? (See **Channels.**) Consider modifying or creating an entirely new **Value Provided** together with your **Customer**.

Who Helps You

Questions	Solution Starting Points
Who are your **Key Partners**?	Could a **Key Partner** take on a **Key Activity** of yours, or vice versa? Could you lower **Costs** by deepening your **Key Partner** relationship, or by making the relationship more strategic? Could you modify or create an altogether new **Value Provided** by allying with a **Key Partner**?
If you lack a **Key Partner**, should you consider finding one?	Could you obtain an important **Key Resource** at a lower cost or with better efficiency/quality by acquiring it from a **Key Partner** rather than seeking it internally? Could you convert/reposition a colleague or someone else as a **Key Partner**? Alternatively, should you eliminate an existing **Key Partner**?

What You Get *What You Give*

Revenue and Benefits Questions	Solution Starting Points
Revenue and Benefits are generated by successfully **Providing Value to Customers**. Is **Revenue** adequate?	If not, you may need to replace or acquire new **Customers** by adding marketing activities. Does the **Customer's** interpretation of **Value Provided** match your own? If so, consider negotiating a price increase or **Cost** reduction. If not, work through the **Value Provided** diagnosis questions.
Are you accepting low **Revenue** or **Benefits** because you underestimate your **Value Provided**?	Check whether you (or the **Customer**) are equating **Key Activities** with **Value Provided**, or misinterpreting the job-to-be-done. For what jobs are **Customers** truly willing to pay? Work through **Customer** and **Value Provided** diagnosis questions to see if you can boost the worth of **Value Provided**.
Would current **Revenue** received be adequate if hard or soft **Costs** could be reduced?	If so, can you reduce/modify **Key Activities** needed to serve the **Customer**? If not, consider finding a new/additional **Customer**, or revising your model.
Is **Revenue** paid in the manner the **Customer** prefers, or in the manner you prefer?	Could you switch from an employee model to a contractor model? From a retainer model to a subscription model? Or vice-versa? Could you change your service into a product that could be sold, leased, licensed, or subscribed to? Could you receive payment in kind? Could you negotiate receiving **Benefits** that cost the **Customer** little but are valuable to you?

Costs Questions	Solution Starting Points
What are the main **Costs** you incur operating under your current model?	Consider soft **Costs** (stress, dissatisfaction) as well as hard **Costs** (time, energy, money): Can you reduce or eliminate any **Costs** by modifying a **Key Activity** or sharing it with a **Key Partner**? Could any **Key Activities** be reduced or eliminated without adversely affecting **Value Provided**? Could you significantly increase **Value Provided** by investing more in a **Key Partner** or in **Key Resources**?
Which **Key Activities** generate the highest soft **Costs** within your model?	**Key Activities** that generate excessively high soft costs suggest a mismatch between **Key Resources** and **Key Activities**. Revisit Chapter 4.

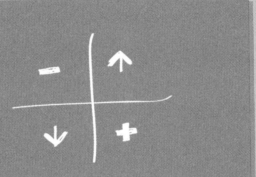

4. Modify Building Blocks and Evaluate Effects

Referring to your responses to the diagnosis questions, list the modifications you'd like to make to your building blocks in the table to the right. For example, if you want to do less selling, in the What You Do row, write "selling" under "Reduce."

For a complete overview of this technique, see the Four Actions Framework in *Blue Ocean Strategy* by Kim and Mauborgne.

Building Block ✏	Add +	Remove -	Grow ⌃	Reduce ⌄
Who You Are and What You Have				
What You Do				
Who You Help				
How You Help				
How They Know You and How You Deliver				
How You Interact				
Who Helps You				
What You Get				
What You Give				

Evaluating the effects of your changes is an intriguing — and sometimes complicated — process. That's because building blocks are interrelated: Changing an element in one building block requires changing an element in another block. We looked at this briefly in Chapter 2, when you painted your organization's Canvas. Now, here's a more detailed primer on making changes and tracing their effects.

How Building Blocks Affect Each Other

Imagine a common problem with the Revenue and Benefits building block: not enough money coming in. You could bring in more money by (1) acquiring more/better/different Customers, or (2) offering a stronger/different/higher-priced Value Provided.

Assume you decide to increase Revenue by adding a new Customer. You would go back to the building block table on the previous page, and in the "Add" column next to Who You Help, describe the new Customer you'd like to add.

So, let's say you've just added a Customer on paper. That's simple enough. But we can't count on new Customers to appear automatically, right? Adding a Customer usually requires additional selling or marketing efforts. Therefore you should make a corresponding entry to **add** or **grow** sales or marketing action next to What You Do.

Building Block	Add +	Remove −	Grow ⌃	Reduce ⌄
Who You Are and What You Have	BRUSH UP SALES, MARKETING SKILLS		SALES OR MARKETING ACTION	
What You Do				
Who You Help	NEW CLIENT			
How You Help				
How They Know You and . . .				
How You Interact				
Who Helps You				
What You Get				
What You Give				

This new entry under What You Do might itself affect other building blocks. For example, if you lack sales skills, you might want to undergo sales training or take a marketing course. You would then make an appropriate entry next to Who You Are as in the table below.

On the other hand, you might accomplish your objective to beef up sales by engaging a partner who is skilled in this area. You would then make an appropriate entry next to Who Helps You.

Here's the trick to effectively revising your personal business model: When you change an element in one building block to achieve a desired result, identify that change's impact on other building blocks. Then, modify elements in those other building blocks accordingly.

Now, go through each building block in your model that needs improving and make appropriate adjustments.

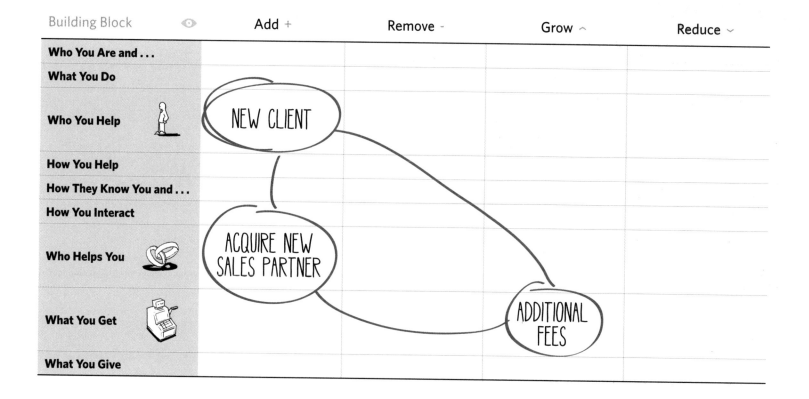

Building Block 👁	Add +	Remove -	Grow ⌃	Reduce ⌄
Who You Are and . . .				
What You Do				
Who You Help				
How You Help				
How They Know You and . . .				
How You Interact				
Who Helps You				
What You Get				
What You Give				

NEW CLIENT

ACQUIRE NEW SALES PARTNER

ADDITIONAL FEES

5. Redraw Your Model

Once you've modified your problem building blocks, it's time to paint a new Canvas.

This is not to imply that you should draw your Canvas once, then modify it once. The Canvas's strength lies in providing a structured way to experiment with different personal business models. It's a way to try out (prototype) different work styles and discover what's best for you.

Prototyping Power

Experimenting with multiple models helps when life changes. What if your terrific manager is replaced tomorrow by the boss from hell? Generating multiple options helps you quickly switch to a workable model that gets you where you want to go.

The Personal Business Model Canvas

Who helps you
(Key Partners)

What you do
(Key Activities)

Who you are and what you have
(Key Resources)

How you help
(Value Provided)

How you interact
(Customer Relationships)

How they know you and how you deliver
(Channels)

Who you help
(Customers)

What you give *(Costs)*

What you get *(Revenue and Benefits)*

Reinvention Inspiration

As personal business model reinventors, we rely on similar tools.
But our individual processes — and outcomes — are unique.

The final pages of this chapter feature four distinctive reinvention stories.
While each differs from your personal circumstances, they may help
enrich and expand your understanding of how you can personally apply
the BMY methodology.

1. Prepare Canvas.

2. In the following stories, note how focus on one
   or two building blocks produced significant change.

3. Redraw your own model.

Remember the occupation index on page 12?
Now might be a good time to review it and read
about an occupation similar to yours.

CHOOSE YOUR CHANNELS

THE MUSICIAN

Following a successful television appearance at age 17, Amsterdam-based singer Hind was signed by German music giant BMG, sold 40,000 copies of her debut album, and received an Edison Award for best upcoming artist. After that, though, she became overshadowed by bigger BMG stars and struggled to promote her own material.

At the same time, the exploding popularity of downloadable songs weakened the traditional music industry business model: Record labels no longer dominated the channels for promoting and delivering music.

Hind realized that coping with the rapidly evolving music industry — and winning the freedom to pursue her own vision — meant she needed to reinvent her personal business model. Hind started asking tough questions about the Channels building block. How did fans find out about her? Was her music purchased and delivered in ways fans preferred? What follow-up efforts ensured listener satisfaction?

Answering these questions lead to a clear decision: Hind and manager Eddie Tjon Fo would create their own label, B-Hind, a new model that would ensure full control over creating, promoting, and distributing Hind's music.

NAME **HIND**

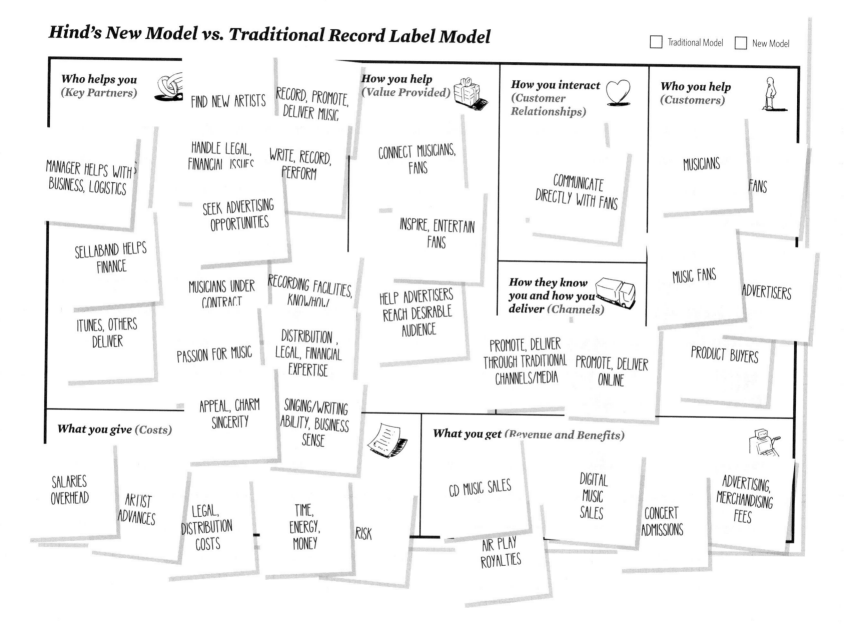

Hind's New Model vs. Traditional Record Label Model

☐ Traditional Model   ☐ New Model

Who helps you (Key Partners)

FIND NEW ARTISTS

RECORD, PROMOTE, DELIVER MUSIC

MANAGER HELPS WITH BUSINESS, LOGISTICS

HANDLE LEGAL, FINANCIAL ISSUES

WRITE, RECORD, PERFORM

SEEK ADVERTISING OPPORTUNITIES

SELLABAND HELPS FINANCE

MUSICIANS UNDER CONTRACT

RECORDING FACILITIES, KNOW/HOW

ITUNES, OTHERS DELIVER

PASSION FOR MUSIC

DISTRIBUTION, LEGAL, FINANCIAL EXPERTISE

How you help (Value Provided)

CONNECT MUSICIANS, FANS

INSPIRE, ENTERTAIN FANS

HELP ADVERTISERS REACH DESIRABLE AUDIENCE

How you interact (Customer Relationships)

COMMUNICATE DIRECTLY WITH FANS

How they know you and how you deliver (Channels)

PROMOTE, DELIVER THROUGH TRADITIONAL CHANNELS/MEDIA

PROMOTE, DELIVER ONLINE

Who you help (Customers)

MUSICIANS

FANS

MUSIC FANS

ADVERTISERS

PRODUCT BUYERS

APPEAL, CHARM SINCERITY

SINGING/WRITING ABILITY, BUSINESS SENSE

What you give (Costs)

SALARIES OVERHEAD

ARTIST ADVANCES

LEGAL, DISTRIBUTION COSTS

TIME, ENERGY, MONEY

RISK

What you get (Revenue and Benefits)

CD MUSIC SALES

DIGITAL MUSIC SALES

CONCERT ADMISSIONS

ADVERTISING, MERCHANDISING FEES

AIR PLAY ROYALTIES

HELP OTHERS, HELP YOURSELF

THE BLOGGER

"For years, I was a compulsive spender," says J.D. Roth. "But when my wife and I bought a century-old farmhouse, I finally hit rock bottom. I'd run out of money." J.D., who sold custom-built cardboard boxes, had always been interested in self-improvement and writing. Now, broke and in debt, he decided to reinvent himself.

He read everything he could about personal finance and summarized his findings in a blog post titled *Get Rich Slowly!* The online essay — and J.D.'s personal commitment to abide by its message — resonated with readers. A year later he launched a personal finance blog, also called *Get Rich Slowly*. "It never occurred to me that a person could make a living by blogging," he recalls. "I just thought I was helping people."

But his online income grew, and before long *Get Rich Slowly* earnings rivaled J.D.'s box company salary. That's when he applied his new personal business model as a professional blogger — and quit his day job. "It was the best decision of my life," says J.D. "I repaid my debt, saved for the future, and helped other people."

But a seven-day-a-week posting schedule and constant interaction with more than 60,000 readers caused J.D. to start burning out. *Get Rich Slowly's* quality began to suffer. J.D. recognized that his personal business model had to evolve again. He found a business partner and hired staff writers so that he could "guide the boat without being the only crew member." The move increased dollar costs, but dramatically reduced J.D's stress and time commitment. That freed him to write for print publications, which boosted both revenue and satisfaction. In the meantime, *Get Rich Slowly's* subscribership continued to grow. Now, J.D. enjoys more time for friends and family, and has achieved long-cherished travel goals, taking extended trips to Africa, Europe, and elsewhere.

"The personal Business Model Canvas helps me, because we all have fleeting thoughts about what we want to do, but we fail to record them," he says. "When you write them down, they become permanent. The Canvas helps you be intentional about what you want to do."

NAME **J.D. ROTH**

J.D.'s Model v. 1.0: Box Salesman

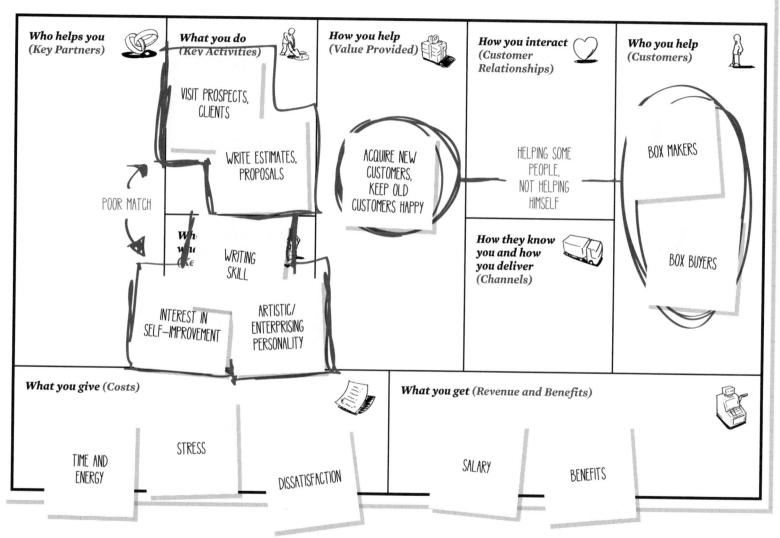

Who helps you *(Key Partners)*

What you do *(Key Activities)*

VISIT PROSPECTS, CLIENTS

WRITE ESTIMATES, PROPOSALS

POOR MATCH

Who you are *(Key Resources)*

WRITING SKILL

INTEREST IN SELF-IMPROVEMENT

ARTISTIC/ ENTERPRISING PERSONALITY

How you help *(Value Provided)*

ACQUIRE NEW CUSTOMERS, KEEP OLD CUSTOMERS HAPPY

How you interact *(Customer Relationships)*

HELPING SOME PEOPLE, NOT HELPING HIMSELF

How they know you and how you deliver *(Channels)*

Who you help *(Customers)*

BOX MAKERS

BOX BUYERS

What you give *(Costs)*

TIME AND ENERGY

STRESS

DISSATISFACTION

What you get *(Revenue and Benefits)*

SALARY

BENEFITS

J.D.'s Model v. 2.0: Blogger

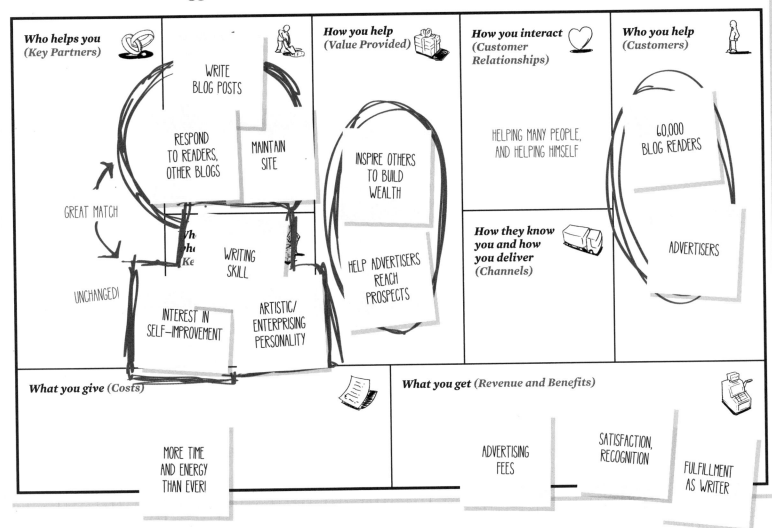

Who helps you (*Key Partners*)

How you help (*Value Provided*)

How you interact (*Customer Relationships*)

Who you help (*Customers*)

WRITE BLOG POSTS

RESPOND TO READERS, OTHER BLOGS

MAINTAIN SITE

GREAT MATCH

Wh... ...h... Ke...

WRITING SKILL

UNCHANGED!

INTEREST IN SELF-IMPROVEMENT

ARTISTIC/ ENTERPRISING PERSONALITY

INSPIRE OTHERS TO BUILD WEALTH

HELP ADVERTISERS REACH PROSPECTS

HELPING MANY PEOPLE, AND HELPING HIMSELF

How they know you and how you deliver (*Channels*)

60,000 BLOG READERS

ADVERTISERS

What you give (*Costs*)

What you get (*Revenue and Benefits*)

MORE TIME AND ENERGY THAN EVER!

ADVERTISING FEES

SATISFACTION, RECOGNITION

FULFILLMENT AS WRITER

J.D.'s Model v. 2.1: Super-blogger

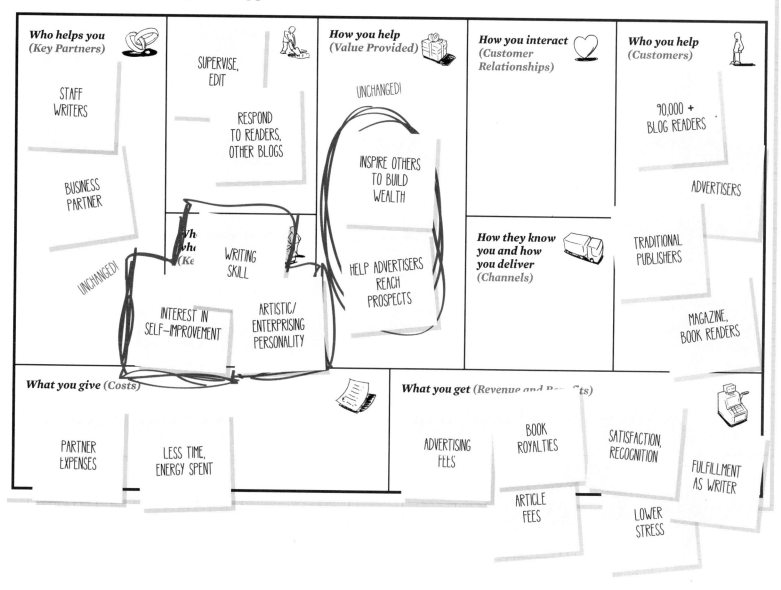

Who helps you
(Key Partners)

STAFF WRITERS

BUSINESS PARTNER

Wh
wh
(Ke

SUPERVISE, EDIT

RESPOND TO READERS, OTHER BLOGS

WRITING SKILL

UNCHANGED!

INTEREST IN SELF-IMPROVEMENT

ARTISTIC/ ENTERPRISING PERSONALITY

How you help
(Value Provided)

UNCHANGED!

INSPIRE OTHERS TO BUILD WEALTH

HELP ADVERTISERS REACH PROSPECTS

How you interact
(Customer Relationships)

How they know you and how you deliver
(Channels)

Who you help
(Customers)

90,000 + BLOG READERS

ADVERTISERS

TRADITIONAL PUBLISHERS

MAGAZINE, BOOK READERS

What you give *(Costs)*

PARTNER EXPENSES

LESS TIME, ENERGY SPENT

What you get *(Revenue and Ben ... ts)*

ADVERTISING FEES

BOOK ROYALTIES

ARTICLE FEES

SATISFACTION, RECOGNITION

LOWER STRESS

FULFILLMENT AS WRITER

UNCOVERING MORE KEY RESOURCES

THE RADIO ANNOUNCER

When Maarten Bouwhuis joined Business News Radio's production department, he hardly dreamed that one day he might become a radio personality himself. But within a few months, he began thinking, "Why can't I work as an announcer, too?" So he made that his goal.

On the way to becoming a radio personality, Maarten worked hard to develop his voice, diction, and interviewing style. And until recently, he considered these and other physical attributes the Key Resources of his personal business model.

But radio hosts earn low salaries, and Maarten started recognizing the limited value of these Key Resources. As time passed, colleague and listener feedback showed Maarten that his interviewing and commentary experience had forged an entirely new set of skills, including the ability to grasp and clarify trends — and a knack for communicating them quickly, clearly, and with emotional power.

These new skills led to work as a discussion leader and facilitator at business seminars and other events. Today, he sometimes earns the equivalent of an entire month's radio announcer salary for a single appearance.

"Never limit your definition of Key Resources to what defined you in the past," says Maarten. "Your personal business model is a work in progress."

NAME

MAARTEN BOUWHUIS

Maarten's Expanded Model

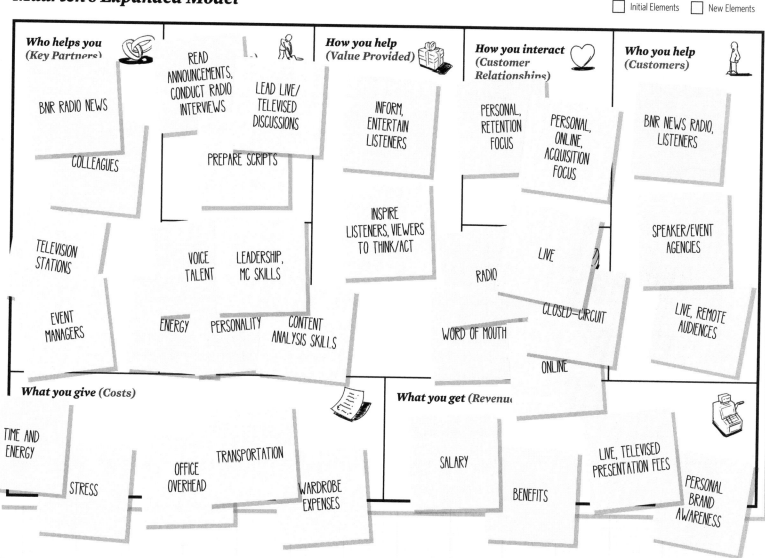

Who helps you
(Key Partners)

BNR RADIO NEWS

COLLEAGUES

TELEVISION STATIONS

EVENT MANAGERS

READ ANNOUNCEMENTS, CONDUCT RADIO INTERVIEWS

LEAD LIVE/ TELEVISED DISCUSSIONS

PREPARE SCRIPTS

VOICE TALENT

LEADERSHIP, MC SKILLS

ENERGY   PERSONALITY   CONTENT ANALYSIS SKILLS

How you help
(Value Provided)

INFORM, ENTERTAIN LISTENERS

INSPIRE LISTENERS, VIEWERS TO THINK/ACT

How you interact
(Customer Relationships)

PERSONAL, RETENTION FOCUS

PERSONAL, ONLINE, ACQUISITION FOCUS

LIVE

RADIO

CLOSED-CIRCUIT

WORD OF MOUTH

ONLINE

Who you help
(Customers)

BNR NEWS RADIO, LISTENERS

SPEAKER/EVENT AGENCIES

LIVE, REMOTE AUDIENCES

What you give (Costs)

TIME AND ENERGY

STRESS

OFFICE OVERHEAD

TRANSPORTATION

WARDROBE EXPENSES

What you get (Revenue)

SALARY

BENEFITS

LIVE, TELEVISED PRESENTATION FEES

PERSONAL BRAND AWARENESS

NAME **NATE LINLEY**

BACKCASTING: AN ALTERNATIVE APPROACH

THE TEAM LEADER

Nate was an electrical engineer who managed a group of software engineers for a global positioning service (GPS) software developer. He was losing enthusiasm for his work, but had trouble defining exactly what was wrong. So he sought help from business coach Bruce Hazen, who suggested Nate try backcasting—envisioning his ideal future career, then "reverse engineering" it to the present.

To begin the approach, Hazen had Nate write four short movie scenes, each depicting himself and two other professionals doing things he found satisfying—things he could see as ideal work.

The scenes were telling: *Nate had cast himself as a leader and builder of teams in each.* What's more, each scenario featured a different setting; Nate had emphasized the details of his team-building roles far more than the industry sectors in which he performed them.

Together, Hazen and Nate "deconstructed" Nate's current and past jobs. What they found matched the theme of Nate's movie scenes: Nate truly enjoyed assembling and managing teams. He loved leading people, helping them think differently about their work, and removing obstacles to their progress.

Nate's backcasting steps

1. Drew ideal model as manager/leader
2. Drew current model as technology manager
3. Rewrote personal story
4. Recognized need to find Customer with world-leading management expertise, reputation for developing managers
5. Sought such a Customer

Just a month after starting his backcasting quest, Nate joined General Electric—a firm renowned for its outstanding management and leadership development programs.

Backcasting means envisioning a desirable future, then working backwards to figure out milestones needed to get there.

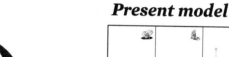

Here are the steps involved:
- Envision and draw your ideal personal business model
- Draw a Canvas depicting your career today
- Identify gaps between your current and ideal models
- Building block by building block, define actions needed to eliminate these gaps
- Execute

"Creating stories about potential futures makes you realize how close to them you may already be."
— Bruce Hazen

Future model

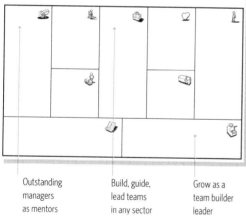

Outstanding managers as mentors

Build, guide, lead teams in any sector

Grow as a team builder leader

Nate's true passion — and his future personal business model — had little to do with engineering and software, and everything to do with team building and leadership . . .

Present model

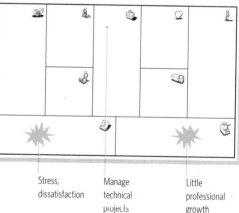

Stress, dissatisfaction

Manage technical projects

Little professional growth

. . . so he rewrote his personal story to recast himself as a manager who engineers rather than as an engineer who manages.

YOUR NEW HYPOTHESIS

So, has working on your personal business model been mostly a paper and pencil exercise until now?

If you're like most of us, it has been. But remember that a personal business model conceived entirely on paper represents a *hypothesis* about your work life — it may contain untested assumptions.

Scientists and entrepreneurs test assumptions by prototyping and experimenting.

We should do the same. So the next chapters cover sharing your Purpose, getting feedback to improve your model, identifying and analyzing potential Customers — and putting your new personal business model into action.

Let's start by considering your "business value" to Customers. Doing so provides powerful insights into how Customers make hiring decisions — and determine salaries or fees.

Act

Learn to make it all happen.

CHAPTER 8
Calculate Your Business Value

What a Paycheck Teaches

As we learned in Chapter 1, all organizations need viable business models, and "viable" means *more cash comes in than goes out* (at the very least, *as much cash must come in as goes out*). This is true for almost all enterprises and individuals. This chapter will help you grasp a key way potential Customers value your services.

To track their performance, organizations use an income statement, an itemized list of sales and expenses. Income statements help organizations understand their operations — and remain viable.

While few individuals use formal income statements, most use similar tools. For example, people balance their checkbooks and use budgets to track bills and paychecks.

Let's learn about income statements by looking at a personal example. Then, we'll see how the same concepts apply to enterprises.

Emily's Income

Emily earns about $4,000 per month as a supply chain analyst at the Giant Shoe Company. After paying bills each month, she manages to save $450, which she deposits into a money market account.[27]

Readers, let's see a show of hands: How many consider pocketing $450 each month a fat profit?

Though $450 seems modest, in business terms, it's more than an 11% profit ($450 divided by $4,000). Few companies are able to save 11% of their income. So believe it or not, on a percentage basis Emily is more profitable than most of the world's corporations!

But "profit" is an unfortunate word. For many, it conjures images of used car salesmen hoodwinking first-time buyers with overpriced lemons, or Wall Street hucksters peddling toxic securities.

Profit and Earnings

We're better served by recognizing that so-called profit is simply the excess of incoming over outgoing funds. In Emily's case, her profit is what she rightfully keeps in return for hard work and good citizenry; it's what she earns for serving her Customers well. It's important to generate earnings. How else can Emily save for retirement, or put aside enough money to send her kids to college?

Similarly, other than by generating earnings, how can a company invest in new facilities or hire additional staff?

Creating just enough income to pay expenses and having nothing left over ("breaking even" in business terms) is a poor formula for individuals or organizations with aspirations beyond mere survival.

"Earnings" and "profits" mean exactly the same thing. But "earnings" is a more appropriate word. Despite the U.S. finance scandals of the late 2000s, the overwhelming majority of corporations work hard to generate modest earnings, just as Emily does. Earnings are either distributed to owners, reinvested in operations, or used to pay off loans.

Does comparing one employee to a large enterprise seem like a stretch to you? You're not alone! As individuals, many of us see ourselves as operating on principles and working toward goals far removed from business practices.

In one sense, that's true. People and companies are certainly different. Nevertheless, as employees, contractors, or entrepreneurs "selling" our services to Customers, it's helpful to think about work relationships in businesslike terms.

The point of this book is to reconceive ourselves as one-person enterprises — enterprises that generate earnings, both for the organizations in which we work and for ourselves.

So!

Let's discuss the ins and outs of earnings. Brace yourself for a bit of math — you'll be well rewarded for the effort.

(IN BUSINESS TALK)
SALES (REVENUE)
− EXPENSES
―――――――
= EARNINGS

(IN NORMAL TALK)
→ MONEY COMING IN
→ − MONEY GOING OUT
―――――――
→ = MONEY LEFT OVER

The Income Statement

An income statement lists three categories from top to bottom: (1) money coming in, (2) money going out, and (3) money left over. In business-speak, these three categories are called Sales, Expenses, and Earnings.

Simple, right?

Corporations create income statements at least once yearly to:

- **Describe their earnings performance**
- **Identify excessive costs**
- **Analyze how sales have grown or fallen over time**

Corporate income statements are more complex than Emily's, but only because they have extra expense categories, allowances for taxes, and other stuff we can happily ignore for the purpose of working on our personal business models. The basic formula is the same:

$$Sales - Expenses = Earnings$$

Take a look at "How Enterprises Use Money" on the following page. You'll see how income statement thinking applies to any organization, whether for-profit, government, or nonprofit.

How Enterprises Use Money

	Businesses	Governments	Nonprofit Organizations
Money coming in	Sales Fees Interest Royalties, etc.	Taxes Bond sales Sales of certain property or services	Donations Gifts Grants Product or service sales (often limited by law)
Money going out	Cost of goods or services sold Salaries Rents Utilities, etc.	Public services: education, healthcare, defense, etc. Social infrastructure Interest payments on bonds issued Public employee salaries, benefits, pensions, etc.	Program costs Salaries Rents Utilities, etc.
Money left over	Earnings (profits) distributed to owners or reinvested in new capacity	Redeem bonds (pay back original amount invested by bond buyers) Invest in additional social infrastructure or services	Invest in program, facility, or staff expansion (ordinarily, nonprofit organizations cannot legally distribute leftover funds to founders or stakeholders)

Take-Home Pay's True Meaning

Take a look at Emily's income statement below. Note that her take-home pay ($2,880) is significantly less than her gross salary ($4,000). Tax withholdings, Social Security, and other payroll deductions — including contributions to her health insurance premium and Medicare — account for the $1,120 difference.

We could think of the $1,120 in payroll deductions as a sort of "cost of income" — an expense Emily must pay as a condition of being both an employee and a citizen (as an employee, she enjoys health insurance and retirement benefits, and as a citizen, she enjoys police and fire protection, free education for her children, and many other benefits).

Naturally, Emily would like to maximize her take-home pay. But she has no choice in the matter: If she wants to earn income as an employee (and stay on good terms with the tax office) she must accept payroll deductions for taxes and benefits. Therefore her cost of income, so to speak, is 28% of her salary.

Now, brace yourself (again!) as we explore the true meaning of take-home pay.

Remember that Emily pays *all* of her living expenses out of her take-home pay of $2,880 — *not* out of her gross salary of $4,000.

This is an obvious fact, but one with crucial implications for understanding enterprise basics (and how your salary is determined). Here's why:

Like Emily, corporations must pay expenses out of their "take-home pay" — whatever's left after deducting costs that *must* be incurred to produce income.

To see how this works in practice, let's examine how the Giant Shoe Corporation creates its "take-home pay."

Emily's monthly income statement

Salary	$4,000
Payroll deductions	1,120
Take-home pay	2,880
Expenses	
Housing	725
Food	600
Medical	125
Car	200
Utilities	175
Other	605
"Profit"	**$450**

A Surprising Truth About Business

Giant Shoe begins by buying the raw materials needed to make shoes at a cost of about $3 per pair.

Next, it assembles the raw materials into pairs of shoes at a cost of about $4 per pair.

Then, it transports the finished shoes to retailers. Let's say this costs about $1.50 per pair.

The cost to make and transport shoes to the place where they can actually be sold totals $8.50 per pair. Now, the retailer buys shoes from Giant Shoe at $22.50 per pair. Giant Shoe therefore earns $14 per pair of shoes sold.

This $14 is called "Gross Margin" or simply "Margin" because it represents how much Giant Shoe has earned after deducting the absolutely essential costs of manufacturing and transport. In a sense, it is Giant Shoe's "take-home" pay: 62.2% of sales. (The retailer will later sell the shoes to consumers at $39.95 per pair — but that's another story for another time.)

Next, Giant Shoe uses its $14 Gross Margin ("take-home" pay) to cover various expenses.

If it plans and executes well and sells all its merchandise, like Emily, Giant Shoe will wind up with earnings, or a surplus.

Here's the crucial point to recall: Giant Shoe Company pays all salaries and other expenses out of gross margin, or take-home pay.

Therefore, to pay Emily's salary expense of $4,000, Giant Shoe needs to generate an additional $4,000 in "take-home pay" (gross margin), right?

Because Giant Shoe only gets to keep about 62% of sales to the retailer, to earn $4,000 in gross margin, it must really generate $6,429 in sales (62.2% of $6,429 is $4,000).

You can easily calculate the dollar amount of sales needed to cover an additional expense — such as a salary — simply by dividing the expense by the gross margin percentage ($4,000 divided by 0.622 is $6,429).

Calculating Your Worth

Imagine you want to work for Giant Shoe at a salary of $4,000 per month. Depending on your worker's benefit package, Giant Shoe will have to cover more than your salary alone. In fact, companies typically contribute an additional 17% to 50% of the amount they pay an employee to help cover health insurance, retirement obligations, state-mandated retirement funding and unemployment insurance, and more. So, let's assume Giant Shoe's contribution is 25% of salary. This means the actual amount of cash needed to pay your salary each month is $5,000.

How's that?

1. **It must have $4,000 to pay you**
2. **It must have 25% of $4,000 — $1,000 — to pay for insurance and other abovementioned costs**
3. **$4,000 + $1,000 = $5,000**

Remember, $5,000 is just the amount of cash Giant Shoe must have on hand each month to cover the cost of having you as an employee. That figure doesn't reflect the higher sales amount the company needs in order to "take home" your salary.

The picture on page 219 shows that, in order to pay a $4,000 salary, the company must sell more than twice that amount worth of shoes.

Note two things about the "How Employees Get Paid" picture.

First, paying your salary requires that the company generate far more cash than what you actually receive.

Second, *all the cash used to pay you ultimately comes from Customers, not from the company.*

Hiring you means Giant Shoe must sell an additional $8,036 worth of shoes each and every month to cover your salary.

So, how will you help the company accomplish that?

This is one secret of business model thinking: *An employee's worth is measured by the Value he or she ultimately provides to Customers.*

When an organization decides whether to hire you, it will consider whether the Value you can offer Customers is greater than the expense of paying your salary.

How Employees Get Paid . . . by Customers

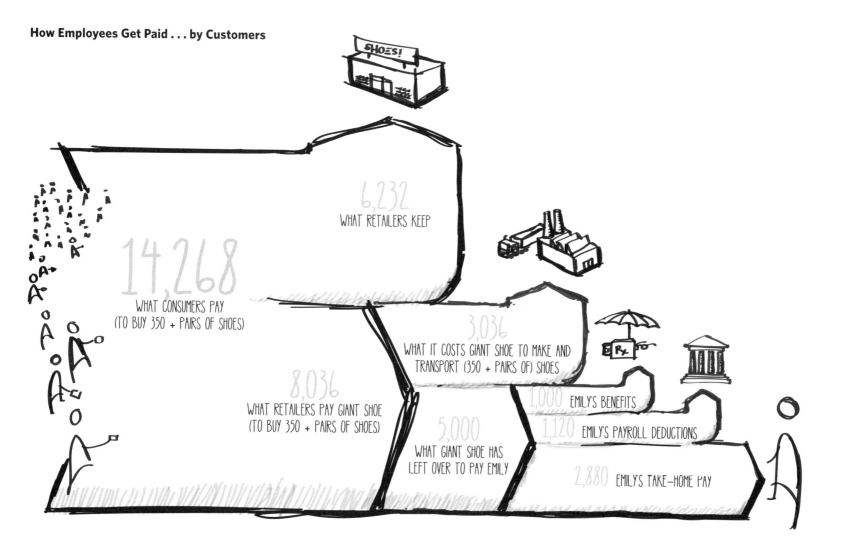

14,268 WHAT CONSUMERS PAY (TO BUY 350 + PAIRS OF SHOES)

6,232 WHAT RETAILERS KEEP

8,036 WHAT RETAILERS PAY GIANT SHOE (TO BUY 350 + PAIRS OF SHOES)

3,036 WHAT IT COSTS GIANT SHOE TO MAKE AND TRANSPORT (350 + PAIRS OF) SHOES

5,000 WHAT GIANT SHOE HAS LEFT OVER TO PAY EMILY

1,000 EMILY'S BENEFITS

1,120 EMILY'S PAYROLL DEDUCTIONS

2,880 EMILY'S TAKE-HOME PAY

Figuring Your Worth

Many corporations don't enjoy gross margins as high as Giant Shoe's 62%. Suppose you work for a company that achieves an average gross margin of 40%.

Q: How much in additional sales would the company have to generate to pay your $4,000 monthly salary? Assume benefits are 25% of salary.

Take-home pay

Benefits

+

"Fully-loaded" salary

Gross margin %

=

÷

Additional sales needed

=

Why Things Are Soooo Expensive

As a rule of thumb, many employers assume that, whatever an employee's salary, the firm must generate twice that amount in additional sales.

Thus, $96,000 in extra sales is needed to cover the full costs of an employee who earns $48,000 annually.

Depending on the industry and/or gross margin percentage, for some employers the rule of thumb is *three times* the annual salary.

When you think about how much it costs a business to operate — and the logic behind determining prices — it's easier to understand why things can be soooo expensive.

Is it any wonder companies obsessively, relentlessly strive to increase their gross margins?

Your Value to an Organization

Put bluntly, if you believe you're worth an annual salary of $60,000, be prepared to explain how hiring you will consistently bring an additional $120,000 to $180,000 into the organization every year.

Of course, nobody's worth is measurable in money terms alone. But employers must make hiring decisions based on weighing the Value you provide to Customers versus the cost of employing you. This is a reason why both companies and individuals need to understand business models.

By now you should have a good sense of (1) how Customers determine your worth to their organization, and (2) how to determine the salary or fees you want to seek. Think about these issues, because it's time to test your personal business model.

Terms to Keep in Mind

Income

Money coming in

Expenses

Money going out

Earnings or profit

What's left over after subtracting money going out from money coming in; same as profit

Income Statement

A summary of an entity's revenues and expenses over a certain period of time, usually three months or a year

Sales

Money generated by selling services or products

Revenue

Sales plus interest, rents, royalties, or other passive income

Gross Margin or Margin

Sales minus the cost of goods or services sold (usually expressed as a percentage of sales)

Cost of Goods or Cost of Sales

The direct cost to the seller of merchandise or services sold

Breaking even

When money coming in equals money going out

Fully loaded (salary) cost

The full cost of an employee's salary, including health insurance (if required), retirement obligations, state-mandated insurance or tax contributions, and so forth, in addition to the salary itself

CHAPTER 9
Test Your Model in the Market

CYD TESTS HER MODEL

THE RECYCLING COORDINATOR

Cyd Cannizzaro had finally defined her Purpose: Help others learn to recycle and to responsibly dispose of trash.

For years, she'd thrived on deep discussions about garbage and recycling with a friend who shared her passion for environmental issues — the two laughingly dubbed their sessions "talkin' trash." But when Cyd was laid off from her job as a customer service trainer, she decided "trash talk" should be more than a pastime; it should be her vocation. Cyd vowed to find work teaching others about recycling — "work that makes a difference," she called it.

Cyd immediately started testing her new personal business model idea.

She was unable to find **Customers** willing to pay for recycling training services, so she revisited her plan and took a job in the deli of a local organic grocery store to improve her knowledge about responsible waste disposal.

Because she was unaffiliated with a recycling organization, she created a memorable "Talkin' Trash" calling card that defined her **Purpose**.

To learn about the requirements for a new personal business model in the recycling field, she started attending green product conventions, public forums on solid waste disposal, and community recycling meetups.

Following interest in her "Talkin' Trash" message from one organization to another, Cyd **tweaked her model** in response to feedback from the industry professionals she met and took on projects closer to her Purpose. One day, her message resonated with members of a municipal task force on sustainability.

Now Cyd Cannizzaro works happily as a full-time recycling coordinator for a city near her home.

Does Your Model Match Customer Reality?

If, like Cyd, you're planning a significant career change, it's important to test the requirements and viability of your model. On paper, a personal business model contains a number of invalidated hypotheses within its building blocks: *It's an untested proposal to help others while doing good things for yourself.*

You test your personal business model by finding, talking to, then acquiring the Customer(s) you want. The best way to test is the way savvy entrepreneurs test new product or service business models: by talking to prospective Customers.

We recommend adapting the process developed by serial entrepreneur and startup guru Steven Blank, who describes how to figure out what Customers need and are willing to buy. This objective, repeat-able process is important because many companies (and unsuccessful entrepreneurs) focus on developing and selling services or products before thoroughly understanding Customers.[28]

For instance, when Motorola failed to discover whether Customers wanted a global, satellite-based mobile telephone system, it lost $5 billion (yes, *billion*) developing and launching its Iridium service. Similarly, R.J. Reynolds lost $450 million on its Premier and Eclipse smokeless cigarettes: Nonsmokers loved the idea — but Customers (smokers!) couldn't have cared less.

Smart entrepreneurs thoroughly test and evaluate their organizational business models before they execute. We'll do well to follow their example and validate our *personal* business models.

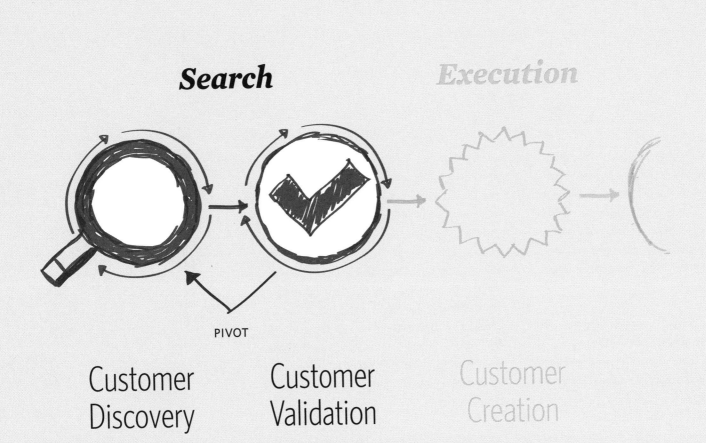

Search

Execution

PIVOT

Customer
Discovery

Customer
Validation

Customer
Creation

How to Test a Business Model

Meet with prospective Customers to test the assumptions (hypotheses) in the building blocks of your one-page personal Business Model Canvas. If Customer feedback suggests changes are needed, go back and modify the appropriate building blocks (this is called "pivoting"). Repeat this process with other prospective Customers.

When your model seems right, try validating it by "selling" to a Customer. If they don't buy, pivot again and modify your model based on reasons given for not buying. When a Customer buys, you are either employed—or ready to create other, new Customers as an entrepreneur.

Get Out!

Customer Discovery begins with what Steve Blank calls "getting out of the building." Career professionals call it "networking." They mean the same thing: contacting and meeting with potential Customers, experts, or people who can introduce you to potential Customers or experts — and discovering whether or not your model is workable.

Remember, your model's building blocks contain multiple assumptions (hypotheses). Each building block within your Canvas needs to be Customer-tested. For example:

- Are Customers confident you possess the Key Resources and/or Partners needed to deliver the promised value? Do your proposed Key Activities support the Value Provided?

- Do any Customers care about the job you want to help with? Are they willing to pay for help as set forth in the Revenue block of your model? (Cyd found no such Customers at first.)

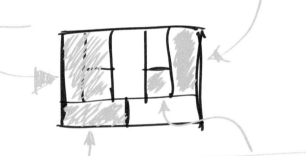

- Can you bear the Costs needed to implement your model?

- Through which Channels do Customers want to be contacted and served? Are you proposing appropriate Customer Relationships?

These questions can only be answered by meeting with potential Customers where they live and work.

The key to effective Customer Discovery is to avoid "selling." Your meetings should focus on validating your personal business model assumptions *from the Customer's perspective*. As Blank says, don't try to convince Customers that they have the problems or opportunities you think they do!

Start with friendly first contacts: Talk with family, friends, neighbors, colleagues, church or professional association members, and others in your personal network. Tell them you're reinventing your career around new goals.

Ask them if they know anyone who might have a professional interest in your goals. Get as many names and contact particulars as you can. These newly obtained names are your referrals.

Next, **contact your new referrals**. The basic principle is to approach people through "warm" contacts — friends of friends, or at least acquaintances of acquaintances. Avoid "cold calling" — approaching people without an introduction.

"Everything great that happens in your career always starts with someone you know. You don't need to surf the 'net. Your next big break will not come from some mysterious technology, or discovery of new information. Your next big break will come from someone you know. Go know people." — Derek Sivers

Most professionals are interested in talking with other professionals about topics of mutual interest.

So pick up the phone, call, and make an appointment. If the other party sounds hesitant or asks for details, **show them how they can benefit from meeting with you**:

I thought you could offer some insight into this issue, and in exchange I'd be happy to share some original ideas and my perspective on the future of sustainable logistics. Would late afternoon next Tuesday or Wednesday suit you?

If she agrees, schedule the meeting. If not, ask her for a referral, thank her for her time and move on.

That's all there is to it. Many people find this kind of calling difficult — even agonizing. *But if you make ten calls like this, things will happen.*

Contacting a referral for the first time?

Take a deep breath, pick up the phone, and try language along these lines:

Hello, Maryellen, this is Emily Smith. I was referred to you by Sally McCormick. I'm a logistics professional keen on new ways of implementing sustainability practices organizationwide. I understand you're an expert in this area, and I'm intrigued to know more about how you and Prospect Company address this issue. Would you have 20 minutes to get together for coffee sometime next week, maybe Tuesday or Wednesday in the late afternoon?

Exhale. Relax. Wait for the reply. If you've spoken sincerely, you'll get a positive response.

Go Further

Here are some prompts to jump-start the discussion and help you start understanding your interviewee's personal or organizational business model:

"Tell me how you got started in _____ and what brought you to _____ Corporation."

"How are you pursuing your _____ goals today?"

"Who shares your problems and concerns about _____? Customers? Suppliers? Regulators? Community members?"

"How do you measure economic impact?"

If you're lucky, the interviewee may hint or even talk openly about a job-to-be-done, a Key Partner, or another aspect of their model. If so, ask clarifying questions and restate the interviewee's thoughts until she enthusiastically agrees with your inter-pretation (clarify now, because afterwards you'll want to concentrate on researching and preparing a proposal to work with this Customer, not rethinking what was said). The Customer may even ask about your Value Provided or another aspect of your model.

If the interview is going *extremely* well — and depending upon the formality of the situation and the scope of help you might offer — you may want to suggest working together right then and there. If so, be ready to discuss specifics of how you will help, as well as compensation (review Chapter 8).

If you sense a written proposal would be appropriate, tell the interviewee that you have ideas about how to help and you'd like approval to submit a proposal. Deep interest in your prospect's goals — and positioning yourself as someone who can become part of a solution — will bring you and your prospective Customer closer together.

After each meeting, reflect on what you learned. You should better understand your model's viability — and the model of your interviewee's organization.

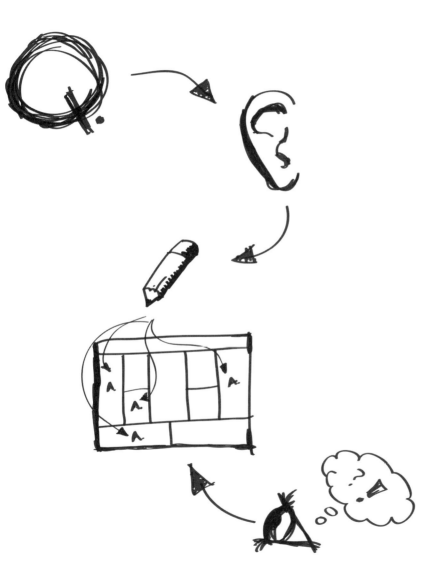

The Secret Question

Here's a question with seemingly miraculous power to elicit deep insights from ordinary conversations:

"What else should I know about . . . ?"

For example, near the end of her interview (p. 229), Emily should be sure to ask Maryellen:

"So, what else should I know about implementing sustainable practices in a company like Prospect?"

Why is this question so powerful? Most professionals harbor pet theories about the challenges, opportunities, and ups and downs of their professions, and they welcome opportunities to share those thoughts. You simply provide the invitation — as a sincere listener eager to hear insights gleaned from your interviewee's hard-earned experience.

Verify Assumptions Within Each Building Block

After each meeting, compare what you've learned with your building block hypotheses. After several such meetings, you should have a good idea which building block assumptions you need to adjust.

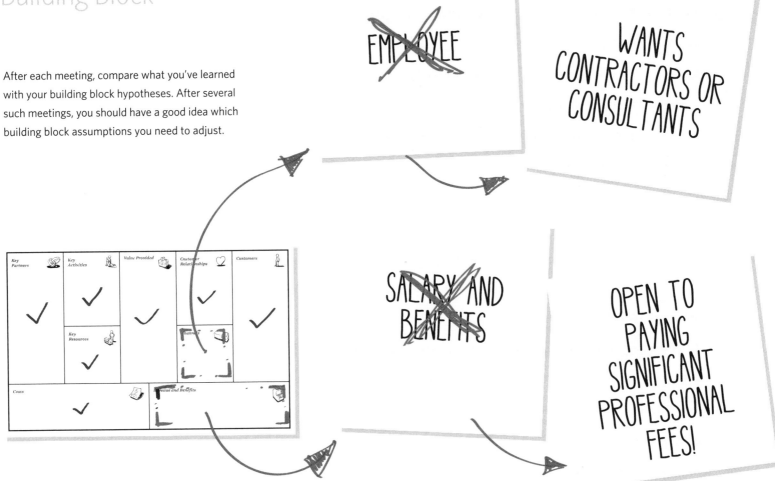

The Entrepreneurship Decision

While testing your model, you may discover that, while you intended to become an employee or contractor, starting your own enterprise is a more desirable option. Conversely, you may discover that, while you intended to start your own enterprise, an attractive employee or contractor position appears.

Either way, you'll face the entrepreneurship decision: Should you start your own venture, or seek to fit your personal business model into a larger organization?

A discussion of that issue is beyond *Business Model You*'s scope, but we'll offer just two thoughts: (1) before deciding to start your own enterprise, be sure to read some of Michael Gerber's earlier work, and (2) most people will find more personal and professional success by *"not"* going into business for themselves. (On the other hand, readers of this book are decidedly not "most people!")

What to Do if Your Personal Business Model Fails to Resonate

When you share your model, do listeners perk up and sit straighter in their chairs? If not, several factors may be at work.

Is your model emotionally compelling? If not, make sure the language you're using is simple, understandable, and appropriate for the professional environment(s) you are targeting. Sometimes good copywriting makes a dramatic difference.

Does your model address real economic problems or opportunities? Few organizations spend money purely for social or political reasons. Rethink how your model can make an economic difference to Customers.

Are you a credible proponent of your model? Can Customers be confident you have the drive, track record, expertise, and skills — the Key Resources — needed to implement your model? If you're unsure how potential Customers perceive you, ask!

The Financial "Plumber"

After being laid off, Jan Kimmell, a seasoned businesswoman with a physics degree, decided her new model would blend finance with operations. The two disciplines rarely go together, says Jan, but they should. Unfortunately, her newly-defined Purpose failed to resonate with informational interviewees.

So Jan developed a memorable elevator pitch:

I'm a financial plumber. I locate leaks and clogs in a company's financial system and partner with operations to make needed repairs and keep profits flowing.

Jan's metaphors may sound corny, but they resonated with new manufacturing sector referrals. Now Jan works for a high-precision manufacturer, blending — you guessed it — finance and operations.

Prepare to Validate Customers

You've found and met with some interesting organizations — some would probably make good Customers. If you feel ready to sell, and are enthusiastic about acquiring a specific organization as a Customer, here are recommended next steps:

1. **Research the organization**
2. **Arrange an interview with a decision-maker**
3. **Propose to help the organization with a specific job**

Ways to investigate prospective Customers include attending trade shows or industry events, talking with experts or analysts, visiting organizations in "adjacent" sectors, and reading professional or popular publications in the prospect's field. Your goal is to put yourself in the prospect's place and learn to see the rest of the world — and *yourself* — through their eyes.

But let's focus on your secret weapon: your ability to recognize, describe, and analyze business models. What better way to understand a prospective Customer than to draw its business model?

How to Obtain "Insider" Data

If your prospective Customer is required to file documents with the United States Securities and Exchange Commission, query the EDGAR database (*sec.gov/edgar.shtml*), a free public resource generally known only to investors, MBAs, and savvy businesspeople. You'll discover an astonishing array of financial and strategic information about your prospect.

Diagram the business models of one or two of the prospective Customers you've identified — and experiment by adding, removing, growing, or reducing different building block elements.

Try to concisely define Value Provided and figure out which building blocks might be pain points. Imagine competitive pressures they may be facing. Could they respond effectively by altering their models? (Incidentally, their competitors may be good prospective Customers, too.)

One surefire pain point is financial: Most organizations are eager to increase Revenue or reduce Costs. Try to quantify — at least roughly — the positive economic effect your personal Value Provided could have on the organization if it were to hire you.

You might start by defining an important job you believe your prospective Customer needs to get done. Then work backwards: What Value Provided would help the Customer with that job? What Key Activities could you perform to create that Value Provided? Do you have the necessary Key Resources? If not, could you enlist the help of a Key Partner? Can you show how external forces are affecting the Customer's business model, and if so, could you help them adjust? Now's the time to unleash the power of business model thinking on behalf of your prospective Customer — and yourself.

The Online Marketer

After graduating, Charlie Hoehn found himself job-less with a "commodity" business degree. Instead of networking through friendly first contacts, Hoehn aimed straight for the top: He cold-called best-selling authors and filmmakers he admired and offered free online marketing services. The strategy worked, and soon led to paying jobs. His client list now includes Seth Godin, Tim Ferris, and Tucker Max.

Sell to a Decision-Maker

Your goal is to meet with and sell your personal business model to a decision-maker in the prospective Customer's organization. Use networking techniques to secure an appointment, but in this interview, focus sharply on a specific aspect of your model that can help your prospect. Your goal is to propose working for the Customer. If the interviewee rejects your proposal, you can pivot and revisit your model.

Approach your decision-maker through the warmest possible referrals. If your networking efforts haven't yet yielded someone who works directly with your potential Customer, by now you should be familiar enough with your target sector to make a connection with a bit more networking.

On the other hand, directly and boldly approaching a decision-maker without any introduction whatso-ever may be the most powerful choice, depending on the industry and/or personalities involved.

When contacting decision-makers you might say something like, "I think you have a significant oppor-tunity to _____ and I have some specific ideas you may find powerful. Can we get together?"

If you've followed business model testing principles up to this point, you're likely to enjoy a warm reception.

Winning Appointments

However you decide to go about approaching decision-makers, these findings from a study by the National Sales Executive Association might change your behavior:

- 2% of sales are made on the first contact
- 3% of sales are made on the second contact
- 5% of sales are made on the third contact
- 10% of sales are made on the fourth contact
- 80% of sales are made on the fifth through 12th contact

So don't give up just because your second, third, or fourth attempt goes unanswered. Persistence wins appointments.

When you meet the decision-maker, state your understanding of the job-to-be-done in general terms, then prompt the interviewee for validation or correction.

If your understanding is correct, the interviewee might say something like, "How would you recommend we solve this problem?" (Just what you want to hear!)

On the other hand, if your understanding wasn't entirely accurate, your interviewee may elaborate on the real opportunities or problems his organization faces. Regardless of how the interview unfolds, stick to your goal of proposing to help.

Depending on circumstances and the formality of the situation, you could make a verbal or written proposal to help.

If the interviewee accepts your offer to submit a written proposal, promise to deliver the document in a week or less. Then thank the interviewee and exit gracefully. Be sure to follow up with a brief "thank you" e-mail confirming (1) the agreed-upon nature of your proposal, and (2) when you will deliver it.

If the interviewee declines your offer to help, it's time to approach a different prospective Customer. If multiple prospects decline your offer, it may be time to pivot and revise your personal business model to better meet Customer needs.

The One-Page Proposal

Decision-makers love brevity and concision, so make your proposal compelling by summarizing it on a single page. Important note: Your concise, single-page overview must signal a reserve of detail you can later present either in person or in a longer document.[29]

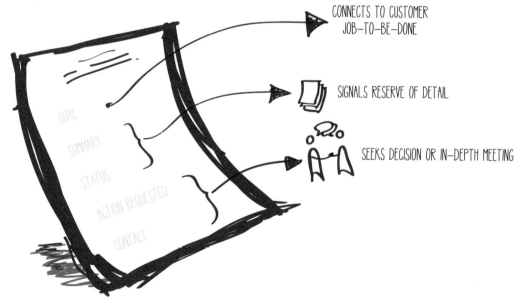

GOAL
SUMMARY
STATUS
ACTION REQUESTED
CONTACT

CONNECTS TO CUSTOMER JOB-TO-BE-DONE

SIGNALS RESERVE OF DETAIL

SEEKS DECISION OR IN-DEPTH MEETING

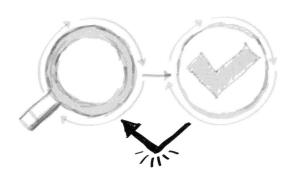

Pivot to Improve Your Model

Pivoting — action you take in response to prospective Customer feedback — means revisiting your model and improving it by modifying one or more building block elements. Pivoting is the appropriate response when you discover your model doesn't yet satisfy Customers.

Your pivot may involve finding an entirely new Customer, as Cyd did (page 224). Or, like Ken, you may decide to modify your Channel (page 62). Then again, you may need to rethink multiple building blocks, the way Dennis did (page 239).

Pivoting returns you to Customer Discovery, where you update your model and once again begin the process of meeting with referrals. When you feel ready to sell your new model, step into Customer Validation mode and try again. Be confident. *You can succeed and will succeed in winning a Customer.*

MATCHING MODEL WITH MARKET

THE COMPUTER TECHNICIAN

Troubled by job stress, Dell Computer technician Dennis Shieh took early retirement to work independently and control his own destiny.

He liked technical work and drew up a personal business model based on buying and running a retail computer store.

Dennis tested his idea by visiting a business broker, who recommended (1) reviewing the financials of computer stores for sale, and (2) taking a personality assessment.

Dennis did both, and learned that (1) computer stores are low-margin, high-turnover operations with poor profitability, and (2) he lacked a consumer-service personality— he was better off focusing on back-room technical tasks and avoiding people-handling responsibilities.

So Dennis pivoted, revamped his model, and replaced consumers with technical business-to-business Customers.

Soon an opportunity arose that Dennis would have dismissed under his first model: a company that sold, serviced, calibrated, and certified commercial scales. The firm met Dennis's needs to exercise technical skills, minimize contact with technically unsophisticated customers, and earn a good, independent living with minimal stress.

Dennis bought the company and now happily enjoys working as a business owner— often in shorts and a T-shirt.

Confidence to Face the Future

When a Customer hires you — or you find the Customer you want — you've validated your personal business model. Now you've arrived at the Execution phase, and your new business model has taken flight. Well done!

You've come a long way. Whether you've done a few of the book's exercises or worked through them all, we hope you'll continue working on your model. At the very least, we hope you've adopted the approach of *modeling* rather than *planning* your work life — of identifying core operating principles that will serve as lasting guides.

You may have noticed that a personal business model is, in a sense, a "relationship map." It shows how **Who You Are** relates to **What You Do**, and how **What You Do** relates to **How You Help**. Most important, it articulates your relationship with **Who You Help** — as well as to the greater communities you serve through your **Purpose**.

Much as a good map guides explorers for years to come, the personal business model methodology can serve as a repeatable pattern for work/life success.

CHAPTER 10
What's Next?

More Ways to Apply the BMY Methodology

Career change is sometimes involuntary. When an organization modifies its business model, employees often need to adjust their personal business models, too. Case in point: Forum member Makis Malioris.

A longtime manager of programmers and analysts at a large international financial services firm, Makis served just one Customer: the head of his Athens office. But career-changing opportunity called when Makis was asked to serve eight new locations, all outside Greece — meaning frequent, extensive air travel. Makis struggled to subdue his first thought: *I'm afraid of flying*.

The new position compelled Makis to reinvent his personal business model. Though he had little intercultural experience, he immediately acquired eight new international Customers, all in different countries, all with different work cultures, styles, and ethics.

Competent and comfortable planning and coordinating the work of close colleagues, Makis now had to convince new Customers to adopt and maintain Information Technology Infrastructure Library (ITIL) processes. This demanded new Key Activities, including "selling," frequent flying, lengthy hotel stays, and replacing face-to-face Customer Relationships with e-mail and telephone calls.

The new position offered a modest increase in Revenue, but huge professional development Benefits. The biggest, says Makis, was international exposure—

and the opportunity to serve as a "process" owner rather than simply a manager. He succeeded in his new role and advanced to an even more responsible position.

Unfortunately, the Greek financial crisis intervened and forced his employer to offer Makis a severance package, which he accepted. But the business model lessons he learned continue to serve him well.

"The personal business model concept helped me identify what I needed to fulfill the requirements of my new role, as well as fill in the gaps throughout each block of the Canvas. It was a demanding situation, but it paid off," Makis says. "Not only that — I'm no longer afraid of flying."

As Makis would agree (and as discussed in Chapter 1) business model innovation — organizational and personal — never stops. Models work for a few years, or sometimes longer, until change is demanded. Your personal business model is certain to evolve again, if not in response to changing times, at least in response to the more experience you reveal in passing years. When the time comes for you to draw a new picture of your work, we hope you'll find *Business Model You* enlightening and inspiring once again.

Here are other ways to apply the **Business Model You** *methodology:*

Teaching business, personal finance basics

Instructors worldwide are using the Business Model Canvas to teach strategy, entrepreneurship, and design, mostly in graduate level business programs. We believe the Canvas is an ideal tool for teaching business basics in undergraduate programs as well. It's a clear, readily understandable way to learn the fundamentals of enterprise-building. Similarly, we believe the personal Business Model Canvas could be a powerful tool for teaching career and/or personal finance fundamentals to high school students.

Career coaching tool

Many of our Forum members have already discovered the power of the personal business model as a coaching tool. A number of the profiles presented in *Business Model You* are living examples of their work.

Individual counseling tool

Page 96 discusses creating Canvases to describe non-work life roles such as spouse, friend, and parent. A number of Forum members have reported success using the Canvas this way. Professional counselors may be able to develop powerful client exercises based on drawing and examining such truly personal Canvases.

Annual reviews/personnel development in organizations

For personnel directors conducting annual reviews, the personal business model could provide a structured way to examine how employees add value to the organization. Enlightened enterprises might extend use of the personal Canvas to helping employees create more value in their off-work hours.

Software support for personal business models

Working with paper, posters, markers, and Post-it notes is powerful and fun, but sometimes a little software support can bring you to an entirely new level. With the Business Model Toolbox for the iPad and the Web, you can sketch out, estimate, annotate, share, collaborate, iterate and pivot all your business models. With the toolbox you get the speed of a napkin sketch and the smarts of a spreadsheet in one.

The toolbox also lets users modify building block labels and content to accommodate personal business model descriptions. A dedicated personal business model application might offer electronic versions of this book's tools to help users assess their interests, skills and abilities, and personality tendencies (Key Resources).

Get your free account and build your personal business model online at www.businessmodeltoolbox.com

Finally, accept our apologies for what in retrospect may seem like a misleading subtitle. If you've gone through even a portion of the exercises presented in *Business Model You*, you've used dozens of sheets of paper applying our "one-page method." But wouldn't you agree the results have been outstanding?

A final word: The conversation continues at **BusinessModelYou.com**, where our book began. Consider joining us there and at **BusinessModelHub.com**, the world's leading community devoted to organizational business model thinking.

Extras

Read more about the people and
resources behind *Business Model You*.

The *Business Model You* Community

This book was co-created by 328 professionals from Argentina, Australia, Austria, Belgium, Brazil, Canada, Chile, China, Colombia, Costa Rica, Denmark, Estonia, Finland, France, Germany, Greece, Hungary, Ireland, Italy, Japan, Jordan, South Korea, Mexico, New Zealand, Nigeria, Norway, Panama, Paraguay, Poland, Portugal, Romania, Singapore, South Africa, Spain, Sweden, Switzerland, The Czech Republic, The Netherlands, Turkey, The United Kingdom, The United States, Uruguay, and Venezuela. Their insight, support, and global perspectives make the personal business model movement soar.

The complete list of co-creators appears on pages 8–9 (some of their photographs appear on the inside covers, in no particular order). We'd like to give special thanks to the following co-creators who made particularly potent contributions to the book:

Jelle Bartels, Uta Boesch, Steve Brooks, Ernst Buise, Hank Byington, Dave Crowther, Michael Estabrook, Bob Fariss, Sean Harry, Bruce Hazen, Tania Hess, Mike Lachapelle, Vicki Lind, Fran Moga, Mark Nieuwenhuizen, Gary Percy, Marieke Post, Darcy Robles, Denise Taylor, Laurence Kuek Swee Seng, Emmanuel Simon, **and** James Wylie.

At **BusinessModelYou.com** you'll find discussion forums, printable Canvases, and most important, a friendly community of readers enthusiastic about improving their work and personal lives through business model thinking. Membership is free.

And please consider joining **BusinessModelHub.com**. With more than 5,000 members, it's the world's leading online community devoted to organizational business model thinking. Membership is free.

Creator Bios

Tim Clark, Author

Tim Clark leads the personal business model movement at *BusinessModelYou.com*. A gifted teacher/trainer and a former entrepreneur who draws on personal experience with multimillion dollar acquisitions and flops alike, Clark has authored or edited five books on entrepreneurship, business models, and personal development, including the international bestseller *Business Model Generation*. He holds master's and doctorate degrees in business, and is currently serving as a visiting professor at the University of Tsukuba in Tokyo.

TimClark.net

Alex Osterwalder, Collaborating Author

Alexander Osterwalder is an entrepreneur, speaker, and the lead author of global bestseller *Business Model Generation*, coauthored by Professor Yves Pigneur with contributions from 470 collaborators in 45 countries. Alexander speaks frequently for Fortune 500 clients and has guest-lectured at top universities including Wharton, Stanford, Berkeley, IESE, and IMD. He holds a PhD from HEC Lausanne and is a cofounder of enterprise software firm Strategyzr and The Constellation, a not-for-profit organization dedicated to eliminating HIV/AIDS and malaria worldwide.

BusinessModelGeneration.com

Yves Pigneur, Collaborating Author

Dr. Yves Pigneur has served as Professor of Management Information Systems at the University of Lausanne since 1984, and as visiting professor at Georgia State University, Hong Kong University of Science and Technology, and the University of British Columbia. He is editor-in-chief of the academic journal *Systèmes d'Information and Management (SIM)*, and together with Alexander Osterwalder authored the international bestseller *Business Model Generation: A Handbook for Visionaries, Game Changers, and Challengers*. He earned his doctoral degree at the University of Namur, Belgium.

Megan Lacey, Editor

Champion of language and running evangelist, Megan joined the *Business Model You* team while reinventing her career. After serving for several years as a publishing company editor, a short but glorious stint as a college writing instructor convinced her to pursue additional teaching credentials. Megan's now completing her Master in Teaching degree at Washington State University, training for her third ultramarathon, and will soon — economy willing — teach high school English (and preach running on the side!).

Alan Smith, Creative Director

Alan is a design-trained entrepreneur whose work has spanned film, television, print, campaign development, mobile applications, and multi-billion-datapoint-per-day Web platforms. After graduating from the York Sheridan Joint Program in Design, Alan cofounded The Movement, growing it into a celebrated international "change agency" with offices in Toronto, London, and Geneva. He has since cofounded Strategyzr, an enterprise software firm that builds ground-breaking practical tools to help people and organizations drive business strategy and create growth.
BusinessModelGeneration.com

Trish Papadakos, Designer

Trish has been committed to a life of visual creation from the day she first put crayon to paper. Following studies at three leading Canadian art and design institutions, she completed her Master in Design in London, England, then founded The Institute of You, a subscription-based career growth service for restless professionals. An avid foodie, photographer, traveler, and entrepreneur, Trish has spent years collaborating with artisans, chefs, and thought leaders.
flavors.me/trishpapadakos

Patrick van der Pijl, Production Assistance

Patrick is the founder and CEO of Business Models Inc., an international business model consultancy based in Amsterdam. He helps entrepreneurs, senior executives, and their teams design better businesses, using visualization, storytelling, and other business modeling techniques. Patrick served as Producer of the international bestseller *Business Model Generation*.
BusinessModelsInc.com

Notes

1 — **Page 8** Everyone profiled in *Business Model You* was interviewed by an author or contributing coauthor. In a few cases, profilee names and/or images have been changed for privacy reasons.

2 — **Page 20** Manpower Group Survey, November 2010

3 — **Page 21** Alexander Osterwalder and Yves Pigneur, *Business Model Generation* (Hoboken, NJ: John Wiley & Sons, 2010), 14.

Page 67 Photo by David White

4 — **Page 51** "Revenue at Craigslist Is Said to Top $100 Million," The New York Times, 6/9/2009.

5 — **Page 85** Richard N. Bolles, *What Color Is Your Parachute?* Ten Speed Press, 2011

6 — **Page 88** Marcus Buckingham, *Go Put Your Strengths to Work*, Free Press, 2007

7 — **Page 90** Tom Rath, *Strengthsfinder 2.0*, Gallup Press, 2007

8 — **Page 91** George Kinder, *Lighting the Torch: The Kinder Method™ of Life Planning*, FPA Press, 2006

9 — **Page 93** Reproduced with permission from Richard N. Bolles, *What Color Is Your Parachute?* Ten Speed Press, 2011, p. 181

10 — **Page 99** Kathy Kolbe posits a fourth factor: will ("conation"). Her Kolby Index is used by many organizations.

11 — **Page 109** This exercise was adapted from John L. Holland's *Making Vocational Choices: A Theory of Careers*, Prentice-Hall, 1973, with help from chartered psychologist Denise Taylor and Dr. Sean Harry, both Forum members.

12 — **Page 109** John L. Holland, *Manual for the Vocational Preference Inventory*

13 — **Page 109** Strictly speaking, Holland's theory allows for 720 (6 x 5 x 4 x 3 x 2 x 1) unique personality "types."

14 — **Page 121** Other ways to obtain similar feedback include engaging a career counselor and using a Web-based service such as Checkster.com. Special thanks to Forum member Denise Taylor for her help with these exercises.

15 — **Page 126** Alain de Botton, *The Pleasures and Sorrows of Work*, Pantheon, 2009

16 — **Page 126** Ibid

17 — **Page 128** Leil Lowndes, *How to Talk to Anyone*, McGraw-Hill, 2003

18 — **Page 140** Adapted with permission from David Sibbet, *Visual Meetings*, Wiley, 2010

19 — **Page 153** Carmine Gallo, *The Innovation Secrets of Steve Jobs: Insanely Different Principles for Breakthrough Success*, McGraw-Hill, 2010

20 — **Page 153** English translation by Allen Miner

21 — **Page 163** Srikumar Rao presentation at Google, April 11, 2008, reproduced with permission

Page 160 Photo of Srikumar Rao by Paresh Gandhi

22 — **Page 166** Srikumar Rao, *Are You Ready to Succeed?* Hyperion, 2006

23 — **Page 168** Rosamund Stone Zander and Benjamin Zander, *The Art of Possibility*, Harvard Business School Press, 2000

24 — **Page 170** Ibid

25 — **Page 173** Alexander Osterwalder and Yves Pigneur, *Business Model Generation*, Wiley, 2010

26 — **Page 176** Ellen McGirt, "Al Gore's $100 Million Makeover," *Fast Company*, July 1, 2007

Page 176 Photo of Al Gore from World Resources Institute Staff

Page 196 Photo of J.D. Roth by Amy Jo Woodruff

27 — **Page 211** Emily is a real person with a different name.

28 — **Page 225** See *The Four Steps to the Epiphany* by Steven Blank for a comprehensive treatment of his Customer Development Model.

29 — **Page 237** Preparing an effective single-page proposal requires significant effort and is beyond the scope of this book — see Patrick Riley's *The One-Page Proposal* for detailed guidance.